How to Play Baseball

How to Play Baseball

*A Parent's Role in
Their Child's Journey*

Chuck Schumacher

How to Play Baseball
© 2014 Chuck Schumacher

Cover and author photos by Will Jordan
Father and son models on cover: Bo and Mason Russell,
photographed at The Ballfields at Liberty Park, Franklin, Tennessee

Trade Paperback ISBN: 978-1-939447-42-5
E-book ISBN: 978-1-939447-43-2

Printed in the United States of America

Dedication

To my parents who showed me "the way" on our family farm. Thank you for playing your role so well—you cracked the whip when necessary; you provided instruction when needed; you cared—always.

Contents

Foreword

Most people know me as a comedian, actor, and writer. Or they don't know me. So, the question is: Why am I writing a foreword to a book about baseball? I understand the confusion, so let me explain.

First, this is more than a book about baseball. It's also a philosophical book in which the qualities and the behaviors necessary to achieve excellence in baseball become a metaphor for all areas of life. Secondly, I've known the author, Chuck Schumacher, for 35 years. He's one of the most special people I know—a master, full of integrity, intelligence, wit, focus, discipline, and who is deeply centered. He's the one to talk to when you need some just plain, grounded Zen-Midwestern conversation. But, more about him later.

I met Chuck in Los Angeles in 1979 when I was at the very beginning of my comedy career. I remember doing yet another late-night spot at the Comedy Store in Hollywood, which meant trying to make eight people laugh at 1:45 in the morning, and then having to face the long, winding drive to the San Fernando Valley, arriving in the driveway of my one-bedroom rental home at around 2:45 a.m. As I pulled myself out of the car, determined to make it inside, so I could get some sleep—and try again another night for eight different people—I looked over to see my yet unknown neighbor pulling into his driveway in a white Chevy van. I thought "What kind of nut is up at 2:45 a.m. just pulling into his driveway?" I watched carefully as my neighbor unloaded music gear out of the van. Clearly, a thief. 'Cause it was way too much gear for me to consider ever moving around at 3:00 a.m.

Unless he was a musician!

Indeed, my neighbor turned out to be Chuck Schumacher, the author of this book, and back then he had a rock-and-roll band that was on the verge of getting a record deal. Of course, Chuck was the sane one who called all the shots while trying to teach four other temperamental musicians about professionalism and discipline. In fact, many of our late-night chats included thoughts about excellence, and what commitment it took. We talked about self-awareness and focus. And, we talked of our path and our calling.

Several years later, after getting to know each other well, Chuck told me, in one of our non-driveway conversations, that he had decided to move to Nashville. Chuck plays a very mean sax, but holding the group of musicians together was too much for him he thought. He was sick of it. I stayed in Los Angeles. having just done my first *Tonight Show* appearance (Chuck was there for that), which changed my life and career, and I had always considered comedy my calling. I knew Chuck had a calling, but I wasn't sure what it was—just that this was a man following his intuition. The quality in a person that I most respect. We kept in touch.

Chuck's wife and two young children loved Nashville. He opened a small karate studio on his property. He was a black belt, and I noticed in Los Angeles that he was very disciplined about his training. Chuck called to tell me that many of the lessons and techniques he had learned in martial arts applied to hitting a baseball. His son was in Little League by this time, and Chuck was coaching. He could take many a young player from a point where they were completely afraid of the ball or swinging too hard to knocking it over the fence and out of the park. Around the ball fields of Nashville there were whispers that he was some kind of wizard. Was this Chuck's calling? To become a master and teach?

A couple of years ago Chuck called me to say "I know this will probably sound odd, but I'm writing a book about baseball." It had been 22 years since he had moved from L.A., and about 18 of coaching little league through high school, evolving into batting coach extraordinaire, and highly respected karate sensei. I could tell that he was on to something. I encouraged him, while at the same time he was getting feedback here and there from some former pro players and a pro scout who were muttering to him "This is it" as he'd shyly show them a newly completed chapter or two.

As I read the chapters, I was stunned by the simplicity with which he could describe complicated human behavior, and what to do. From dealing with angry parents who are too tough on their own kid, to dealing with the coach, other parents, and even the vendors, to kids who would just sit down in right field while the opposing team was at bat, he seemed to know what to do. As he simply likes to call it: *problem-solving*. I sat there with a pile of pages in front of me, and realized that this book was Chuck's calling. It's the sum total of a life led with integrity, depth, courage and wisdom. The wisdom that comes from letting go of all the false beliefs in the mind, and trusting the instinct—the intuition that he always possessed. Strangely, my life and work had moved in the same direction, and that's one reason we've remained friends. I'd always found in comedy that the most difficult thing to do is the simplest thing to do, to listen to that quiet, simple voice that is most often clobbered by inaccurate thoughts and outside noise.

I hope you enjoy this book. I think it's great for parents, kids, and coaches. As for me, I have to get going, because I have an early spot at the Comedy Store—tonight! The only thing I miss about those late-night spots are the 2:45 a.m. driveway chats with Chuck.

And those eight people.

—Garry Shandling

Chapter 1

Baseball: Not Just a Sport

In many ways, a baseball game is an opportunity for us to show our real character.

Can we keep our cool when the umpire makes a bad call? Can we stay calm when our team just blew the lead which they had built up? Can we show patience when our son or daughter is struggling to hit the ball? Can we lose with dignity and win with humility? If you're honest with yourself and the answer to any of the above questions is "no," you're not teaching your kids the most important thing: how to find success in life. It's fun to win the ball game, but we should do our best to master these character traits first. If we can, not only will we be showing our kids how to deal with the realities of a baseball game, but we'll be teaching them to deal with some of life's curveballs as well.

At our workplace, do we rant and rave and publicly disrespect authority when we don't get our way? Probably not; we would likely get fired. We can't afford this kind of behavior because the stakes are too high. Yet, at youth sporting events, you see it from parents of young athletes all the time. Are the stakes not just as high—or higher? When adults display arrogant behavior at baseball games or other youth sporting events, they're not aware of the message which they are sending kids: that when we don't get our way, we whine and complain. These adults are displaying the very kind of behavior which they would claim to be teaching their kids not to display. They know that it's not okay to act irresponsibly at a baseball game. They're just too selfish to keep themselves from doing it. They like the temporary feeling of power which it gives them. The problem with this lack of awareness is that it only serves the adults' needs, not the kids' needs. *The adults' needs are instant gratification; the kids' needs are having fun, constant instruction and, more importantly, a good influence from their parents.* Kids are good mimics. Parents are the ones whom kids will mimic most when they are young. If parents are dishing up a steady diet of poor behavior during baseball games, then their kids can naturally lean toward that same behavior themselves. Why wouldn't they? They love and respect their parents and, at a young age, often assume that their parents are right about everything.

During baseball games, there are countless opportunities to show *good* examples of proper behavior to live your life. It doesn't mean that you're not having fun because you're behaving yourself at a baseball game. One thing is for sure: It does mean that you're *not* embarrassing your child by acting like one yourself.

At the beginning of every season during my coaching career, I (and many other baseball coaches) would talk to our assistants and parents on the team about our philosophy and our expectations for the season. Everyone always agreed on the proper behavior. All the right words were spoken: "It's for the kids," etc. The real test was when the competion began and parents' emotions got involved. This is when we would see which parents were playing their role correctly.

If we pay attention, we can learn a lot about ourselves and grow from the experience of competition and help our young players to do the same (which requires humility). The baseball game gives us many opportunities to display good or bad sportsmanship. Our true character will be on display and it will be apparent to the casual observer if it's "for the kids" or "for the parents." By being knowledgeable about our role as parents, we can show kids that being organized and working together for a common goal will give us a chance for success. Being unorganized usually leads to confusion about goals and it also enables poor communication. Parents not playing their role correctly will take the fun out of it for the kids. The result is predictable: confusion.

Just as in other aspects of life, kids need clarity when it comes to participating in sports.

My favorite thing about baseball is the great opportunity to show kids how to deal with failure, while still enjoying something which they love to do. Baseball is a game of many skills and they take time to develop. When a kid can't perform because of undeveloped skills, they often see themselves as failing. For them, failure happens throughout the whole game in the way of a strikeout, an error on defense, and many other ways. How a player deals with these perceived failures has a lot to do with their ultimate success. How a parent deals with their young player's unsuccessful attempts will either help their child or hurt them.

A parent's attitude is powerful! If a parent is being negative or overbearing, the young player's attention will focus on the parent instead of the game. As kids grow older and more independent, parents will face the consequences of being tuned out completely on and off the field if this negative and overbearing behavior continues. By trying to live up to their parent's expectations, kids will soon realize they are on a failed mission and tend to play it safe so they won't disappoint their parents by making an error on a tough play. Instead of trying for the tough play, they'll let it go. They will be afraid to fail, which will lead to even more failure.

Success may come in the way of winning a game or a tournament. It may also come in the way of a personal realization: that keeping a positive attitude is what will allow you to sustain a good effort. By sustaining a good effort, your child can learn to overcome things with which they are struggling, such as striking out on a regular basis. The ability to sustain a good effort through adversity is far more important than any game or tournament, because games are not always a good indicator of success. Many times in youth sports, I have seen teams win while displaying bad attitudes, arrogant behavior, and poor sportsmanship, while the losing teams put their good character on display even though they lost the game. Who was successful? How parents play their role when their child is experiencing failure or success is what will determine which attitude their child will adopt: negative or positive. If you, as a parent, are teaching your child that their own effort is what they have control over, they will eventually learn this life lesson and give themselves a great chance for success not only in baseball, but other areas of their life as well. This is a very positive approach! If you are the type of parent who thinks that you can control an outcome by yelling at kids, complaining, arguing with umpires, or disrespecting the coach, you are setting your child up for ultimate failure. This is a very negative approach, and it's what your child will learn from you!

Being part of a baseball team can present many challenges for players of all ages. Natural ability, natural desire to learn new things, unique talents, athleticism, work ethic, and attitude will all play a part in how you fit on the team. Every player can grow in their experience, no matter where they fall in these categories. When players are five and six-years-old, many (not all) coaches will give every player equal playing time and a chance to play many different positions. Some leagues don't even keep score at this age. These are good things.

For many kids, this is their first experience with baseball. Here is an opportunity to teach them Life Lesson Number One: Have fun! This lesson should go hand-in-hand with all the other life lessons yet to come as a player continues on their baseball journey. If every recreation league adopted this philosophy, competition at this very young age would take a back seat to skill development, character building, and just plain fun. Young, inexperienced parents would also have an opportunity to clearly see how their child fits in, without the cloud of competition getting in the way and influencing their behavior.

To all the coaches who blurt out ridiculous phrases like "practice shouldn't be fun," I would say, "If kids aren't having fun, good luck trying to get them to focus on the difficult task of developing skills."

Yes, you could do as many coaches and parents do: yell at them until they do it. I have witnessed this many times and, in fact, it does satisfy the need of a coach or parent at that moment (aka "instant gratification"), but it's not a good teaching tool. The kids will respond through intimidation and the only thing that it teaches them is to resent you. I think the reason that this approach is so popular is that *it's easier to yell than it is to be resourceful enough to train kids and have fun at the same time.*

Through baseball, there is a great lesson to learn for parents and coaches when it comes to training kids. The lesson is this: *Arm yourself with knowledge about how to run a practice; take the time to learn specific drills for your age group that will develop skills, and you will find that there will be less yelling and more learning and having fun.*

By becoming informed and prepared, you will be giving kids specific information that can help them be successful and you will be playing your role very well. You wouldn't go to your workplace unprepared. Why would you go to a kid's baseball practice with limited knowledge on how to run a dynamic, fast-paced practice that everyone, even the coaches and parents, can enjoy?

Coaching and organizing youth baseball is a huge responsibility. As a parent, your role may be that of coach, assistant, team mom, scorekeeper, crowd participant, or some other important role. The more organized and knowledgeable we are in these positions, the more our kids will learn about liv-

ing life. They will see that the formula for success on a baseball team is good effort, preparation, and teamwork. You are
ultimately showing them that this is what will help them later
in life with school, jobs, relationships, and one day, raising
their own kids.

Baseball, with its many skills to be developed in order to
have success, and the many opportunities which the game
presents for learning life lessons, truly is more than a sport. It's
a wonderful opportunity to show kids, at an early age, how to
live their lives and learn life lessons, such as:

- Being accountable for your actions. *Example:* A player
  is not paying attention and it results in an error. *Solution:* Just admit it, learn from it, and *choose* to pay attention next time.

- Not making excuses. *Example*: A player strikes out on
  a called third strike and blames the umpire. *Solution:*
  Understand that more work on "two-strike hitting"
  will help you get better. You have no control over the
  umpire.

- Accepting your role on the team. *Example:* A player
  doesn't get to play the position that he wanted. *Solution:* If you have aspirations of playing certain positions, you can increase your own level of effort at any
  time by practicing the skills unique to that position,
  thereby increasing your skills to give yourself a better
  chance in the future. In the meantime, willingly accept where the coach puts you.

- Respect for those who are helping you. *Example:*
  During the pre-season, parents appreciate the coach,
  thanking him for his effort. When the games begin
  and the team is not winning, parents start blaming the
  coach and no longer talk to him at games. *Solution:*
  Remember that he is the same caring coach that he
  was before the competition began. He still deserves
  the same respect. Show him this respect and your kids
  will as well. There are many things a coach has no

control over, such as a player's personal effort, preparation, and attitude. He also has no control over the umpire or the opposing team. If we do not remember this, we are teaching kids how to disrespect people who are trying their best to help them, just because we are not getting what we want. This will not serve you well in baseball, nor in life.

- How to be a team player. *Example:* Be happy for other people's success, not just your own. *Solution:* Remember that it takes the success of many to have a winning baseball team. The same can be said of running a business, or the country.

Our kids are aware of our behavior at practices and games; they're always watching us.

Hopefully we adults have learned the many life lessons that baseball has to offer so we can be role models for our kids whether things are going well or poorly. Whether we are winning or losing we can still find joy in just playing the game and living our lives. When we make the immediate outcome more important than our child's development over time, we can mess up the natural progression of building skills, playing the game for fun, and eventually developing a passion for the game. Once a passion has been developed for something, some real learning can happen quickly. Kids will then be able to get the most out of their ability. If coaches and parents only show joy and positive emotions when the team is winning, kids will start to equate losing the game as failure on their part.

Being a winner has nothing to do with winning a baseball game. If parents do not understand this, they are looking at baseball only as a sport. They will be missing the chance to show their kids that baseball is not just a sport, but a fun and challenging activity that gives them the opportunity to learn skills that will help them for the rest of their lives.

Chapter 2

Attitude

A Parent's Role in Developing a Good Attitude: hold kids accountable for poor behavior and lack of effort.

It's the first game of the season for my team of nine-year-olds. It's a doubleheader. Everyone is excited to play and parents can't wait to see their kids on the field. Ben, our pitcher in Game One, performs well. In spite of errors by the team that led to long innings for him, he kept his composure and pitched well until his pitch count was reached. At this point, he is removed as a pitcher and asked to play center field by the coach. He shows obvious disappointment by drooping his shoulders and lowering his head, and reluctantly walks out to center field. It's early in the season; he's only nine-years-old. I let it go and decide to talk to him about it later. The game ends with a loss, due to bad defense on our part.

Game Two begins.

Ben is again asked to start the game in center field. He displays the same behavior toward another coach, thinking that this time, maybe if he pouts he will get his way and be able to play the infield. Again, we look past it and send him out to center field as planned. Our pre-game plan was to start him in center field and move him to first base after two innings. He's a left-hander and these are positions which he can realistically expect to play as he grows older.

By the third inning, Ben is on the bench, "riding the pine," as they say, and never made it to first base, where he was hoping to play all along. As a center fielder, he is indeed in center field; but, instead of being a team player with a good attitude, he chooses to not pay attention to the game at all. At one point, all three coaches observe him with his back to the batter as the ball is being pitched, instead of watching the ball come off of the bat, as was taught in practice. During the next pitch, he is watching the game, but this time he is down on one knee and never does get up until the catcher returns the ball to the pitcher. That is enough for all three coaches, so we replace Ben with another boy who is sitting on the bench, eager to be in the game at any position.

This scenario is one that happens in similar ways all the time in youth baseball. When kids are young, not only are they learning the physical game of baseball, but they need adults to help them understand how their actions, whether they are good, bad, or indifferent, will directly affect not only their playing time on the team, but eventually other areas of their lives. As a coach, every year I can't help but notice that some players already have a good understanding of this and others do not. I can only assume that they have formulated their attitude based on their experience with those in charge of raising them—their parents.

In this case, the parents just couldn't bear the fact that their child was the first one who had to be disciplined in this way. The mother met me after the game to get an explanation of what had happened, so I explained the situation. Instead of thanking me for taking the necessary action, she decided to criticize my method of discipline, saying that I was inconsistent because I don't "get on the kids" when they don't pay attention at practice. When I explained to her that it is a completely different situation and we do make the kids run a lap or do pushups at practice when they don't pay attention, she responded with, "But you're always so easygoing; I've never seen you do that before." When I said that I had not had to until that moment, a look of sheer terror crossed her face. It now became obvious to me why Ben acts the way that he does.

Two days later, Ben's parents requested a conference call to express their concerns about the situation; they were still upset about it. The conversation was the same as before, with the parents wanting to talk about anything except what had actually happened with their child in the game. They had now come up with other scenarios that would put others at fault in completely different situations, trying to compare them with Ben's actions. At one point they emotionally exclaimed, "Ben is such a good boy!" No one had ever suggested that he wasn't and, by their overreaction, you would have thought that we had kicked him off of the team! I responded with "Our response to his actions was appropriate and he was treated fairly." They finally said, "Let's just agree to disagree."

The conversation continued with them questioning my coaching expertise because, in their words, "we should have won those two games." In a feeble attempt at making this situation about the coaches and the other players, instead of just holding their child accountable for poor behavior, they were setting him up for more of the same in the future. It would seem that Ben had been getting his way at home when he pouted and had not been held accountable for his actions.

Since Ben was a talented player, it's possible that he had been getting his way with previous coaches because they were more interested in winning than in teaching life skills, and felt that they couldn't afford to sit him down. Ben's reaction to my taking him out of the game was positive. He knew that what he did was wrong, and he also knew that I did what I had said that I would do when a player displays a bad attitude, and that a bad attitude is the one thing that will get you on the bench, no matter who you are.

Ben was a great kid and was one of the most naturally talented players on the team, yet he was playing beneath his capability. His parents also displayed a poor attitude by trying to make excuses for him. If this continues, Ben will constantly be getting the wrong message from his parents (who have let their own emotions get in the way of his training), and his coaches (who are willing to overlook his bad behavior so that they can win the game). They will be missing a great opportunity to teach Ben how to win in life, by taking responsibility for his own actions.

The ball field is a great place to teach kids this valuable lesson, with caring coaches and parents, instead of putting it off until later in life by making excuses for them now.

We have another player on our team, Aaron, also nine-years-old, who does not possess these natural physical gifts, but because of excellent attitude and respect, is developing and playing well above his level of natural talent. He gives 100% all the time and is happy to be on the field wherever the coaches ask him to play. Like Ben, Aaron has been a student of mine for about two years. He has great desire to become a good ball player and, because of lesser ability than some, has had to fight through tears of frustration more than once. Baseball is a tough sport in which to excel. But, through patience on the part of his parents and me, we have become partners with Aaron on his baseball journey. Aaron is clearly learning important life lessons: that having humility, staying positive, and choosing to give a good effort will help him in baseball and in life.

It is easy to see that someone, probably their parents, have affected Ben and Aaron in the way in which they behave. If kids are not held accountable for their behavior, they will soon develop the attitude that they are special and deserve special attention. When it doesn't happen, they seek out someone who will give them special treatment. If they are taught to be responsible for their actions, they will learn to thrive in any situation, whether it is on the ball field or in life in general.

Neither of these parents know much about the game of baseball, yet Ben's parents boldly express their opinion on how to coach and teach discipline to someone with twenty years of experience in baseball and thirty-two years of experience in martial arts and training kids! It's a way of taking the focus off of the real issue, which in this case, is the role of the parents in their child's journey.

It's not the end of the world if your child, at nine-years-old, has not learned everything there is to know about baseball, or even if he displays a poor attitude sometimes. Instead of making excuses for young ballplayers, however, we, as adults, are responsible for teaching them to be accountable for their actions and to put our own egos aside so that we can keep a clear head. We must make sure that we are teaching our young players to put forth good *effort* instead of making excuses for them. They will learn whatever we teach them and they will also tend to mimic our behavior (especially if we are their parents), whether it is good or bad.

When my own son was young, we had many conversations about learning life's lessons through baseball, a sport that he loved and still does. Now, as a young adult, I see him displaying these character traits in his professional career and I am thankful for it. When the umpires, players, parents, and coaches come to the baseball field to cooperate with one another for a common good, they are showing respect for each other. When this happens during competition, the only possible result is everyone having fun, win or lose. When it doesn't happen, we all have seen the unpleasant results, whether on the evening news or firsthand on the field.

Failure, unfair treatment, success, and the presence or absence of a good work ethic are all things that a young person will face during their lifetime. Their attitude toward these things, whether it is good or bad, will eventually shape who they are and how others perceive them. If we equate success only with winning the game or having a winning season, then, when it doesn't happen, we are likely to make excuses for our failures, let unfair treatment affect our own efforts, let success go to our heads, and forget that developing a good work ethic is something over which we have control.

Our mindset should be a positive one, even in the face of failure. On our baseball journey we must remember that there will be ups and downs, just as in life. We must not let the downs define who we are. We must teach young ballplayers that a good attitude, combined with good effort in developing their skills, is what will help them on their journey. Their opportunities are ahead of them as others come to realize that they are someone who can be counted on when things are good *or* bad.

And here is the very reason why teaching young players the importance of staying positive, learning self-discipline, and putting forth good effort always are the main goals. In the example mentioned earlier, if Ben had reacted differently, there would have been a much different outcome and perspective for him. As it is, others around him, such as his teammates, his coaches, and other parents, see him as a kid who just pouts when he doesn't get his way. He only hustles when things are going well. Even after the incident in center field, he gives just enough and no more. He did learn that he should not turn his back to the batter or take a knee as the ball is being pitched. I taught him that by sitting him on the bench. (Had I left him in the game, he would not have even learned that lesson.) At nine-years-old, it's hard to blame Ben for this behavior. He's only acting the way that he has been taught to act. If he pouts, he gets his way. If he was taught to act in a more respectful and humble way, the situation could have played out like this:

Ben pitched a great game, in spite of errors by the team that led to long innings for him. He managed to keep his composure and stayed out there until his pitch count was reached. When asked to play center field he said "yes, sir," grabbed his glove, and run out to center field, eager to catch a fly ball, or to help the team in any way that he could. His attitude was impressive! Game Two started and, again, Ben was asked to play center field. He hustled out to his position, because that was where the coach had sent him. He paid

*attention and did a nice job. After two innings, Ben was
moved to first base, just as we had planned before the game.
He hustled into the dugout to get his first baseman's glove
and did his best at first base.*

In this second example, Ben's teammates, coaches, and other parents would now see Ben as an inspiration to the whole team. He showed good character, a positive attitude, and leadership, and knew how to deal with failure by staying positive. All this and we lost the game. Sound impossible? For those who think that real success is winning a game at nine-years-old, yes, it is impossible to see life's lessons that we can learn through competition. It's not about the competition: it's your attitude and perspective towards the competition that count.

As is the case with developing physical skills, developing one's attitude takes time and is directly connected to whoever is teaching these skills. If, when teaching someone how to hit a baseball, your expertise and knowledge are based only on thinking "this is how we did it when we were young," you may be teaching incorrect motions to a young player, who will now repeat those incorrect motions until they become muscle memory. Now you have a problem to solve if they want to play at a competitive level, as on a high school team. The same thing is true when it comes to our actions. If the coaches and parents are not holding players accountable for their poor attitude towards coaches, other players, and the game itself, a young ballplayer's character is likely to become one that lacks humility, and they will feel entitled to everything. In Ben's case, I sincerely hope that his parents will accept the fact that Ben should be responsible for his own actions and that they not cover up for him by blaming others or making excuses for him in the future. If so, I believe that, with Ben's talent and love for baseball, he will develop a good attitude about the game and life, and it will take him far.

Chapter 3
Effort

Parent's Role in an "Effort over Outcome" Approach to Teaching Kids. Most basically, ensure that your language and demeanor reflect this philosophy.

Every spring, my wife Lynn and I go to Florida to watch Major League Baseball's spring training games. I love watching the games, witnessing the best players in the world still putting out the effort that got them there. Before every game, it's inspirational to watch the routine that these amazing players go through to prepare themselves to play against other players of their same caliber. It's motivating to watch some of the best hitters in the world, still accepting advice from their hitting coaches. They know that good effort leads to good results; it has become a habit. These players have not only developed the discipline to show up early, but also the ability to put forth good effort once they get there. They realize that they have no control over what other players do, but only their own effort as a means of helping them win, so they prepare for success. Relatively speaking, kids should be taught this lesson from day one. During spring training games, managers make sure they are using all players, not just the starters. This is important for the development of the team as a whole. After about four innings, the starters are finished for the day and the rookies take the field. This usually happens for both teams and as a result, it remains competitive. When I witness this each year I always think, this is how youth sports competition, especially at the younger ages should be developmental. Once the season begins, the main difference in professional sports and youth sports is revealed: in professional sports, winning is the most important thing; in youth sports, while learning how to win is important, teaching kids to give a good effort while developing physical skill and building character should be front and center!

"Let's not get ahead of ourselves." This is a phrase that you hear from people who understand the value of effort. These people are often leaders who have experienced some success. They know what the ultimate goal is. They also know that focusing *only* on that goal will not get them there. The ultimate goal isn't real. What *is* real is the immediate goal: consistent good effort. By focusing on the immediate goal, the ultimate goal can become real.

When your child is six-years-old and it's their first year of playing baseball, you have no idea how many years they will play. But, as you begin this journey with them, you have a choice as to how you'll proceed. Is it their first year of Little League, or do you see it as the first year of their big-time career in baseball, maybe at a Division I college or as a professional? Many parents proceed as if it's the first year of their child's career in baseball instead of just a fun activity for their child. If this is the path that you take, while you are feeding your ego and living vicariously through your child, your child won't have much fun. It'll seem more like a job to them. Although they won't admit it, when overbearing parents talk to their kids about effort, they mean the effort that it takes to live up to parents' unrealistic expectations. When parents with a proper perspective talk to their kids about effort, they mean the effort that it takes to get the most out of their child's ability.

Chances are, if it's your first child to play sports, you'll be a little unsure about some things as you proceed. Depending on where you live, there may be many options as to where your child can play baseball. Deciding between the local recreational league and the more competitive travel league is a decision with which many parents struggle. Just remember that, either way, it's still your child's personal effort in attitude and skill development that will ultimately make the difference in how they develop as a person and a ballplayer. Being on a winning travel team will not guarantee future successes.

Personal effort in training is the key to future success.

I have seen many players experience success on their travel team when they were twelve-years-old, but fail to sustain it as they mature. Why? On many travel teams, the coach's only goal is beating the twelve-year-olds on the opposing team; character and skill development take a back seat. Many coaches are capable of winning games with *naturally talented* young kids, but are lacking in ability when it comes to teaching techniques that will develop a player's skills, skills that, when repeated over a period of time, will allow players to be able to compete at higher levels in the future. The best coaches are the ones who have a second goal: teaching life lessons through skill development. Even if they don't win as many games, they are helping their players win for their future, which has a lot more meaning than winning the twelve-year-old World Series.

It's hard to develop skills properly when most of your time is spent playing games. Playing an excessive amount of games leaves little time for individual or team practice. The kids also need a break to just be kids and for family activities; otherwise they will get burnt out on baseball. When this happens, we have to ask ourselves why. The misguided efforts of adults are usually the answer; kids don't schedule games. The result of scheduling too many games is this: skill development is retarded in favor of overindulgence in competition. Improper mechanics and lack of rest also puts these young players at increased risk of over-use injuries as their muscles, bones and joints mature, especially before puberty.

No matter what level of talent or interest your child has in baseball, a balance must be struck between competition, personal skill development, and just plain fun! These days, it's common to see travel teams with players as young as six-years-old. In these younger age groups, winning can be easily accomplished if you recruit players who have matured early or who are naturally talented. The worst cases are the teams who outmatch the competition because some parent or coach on the team has the gift of gab and was able to recruit talented players by painting a picture that resembles something from the big leagues. Slick uniforms, matching shoes and bat bags, expensive bats, and warm-up jackets become more appealing to parents and players than skill development.

Many bad habits are developed when the goal is to make superstars out of kids. Proper training will be overlooked in favor of letting players do what is working for them against other inexperienced kids, even if it is weak technique. When these players get older, weak technique will not hold up against players who put more value on skill development when they were younger.

A steady diet of poor or misguided effort on the baseball field will ultimately result in failure. It would be like eating doughnuts every day and never eating anything nutritious. Yes, they taste good, but eventually your health will suffer if you don't make adjustments to your diet. When kids are young, their technique will be poor. The players with natural athletic ability will have success in spite of poor technique, which is why coaches strive to stack their team with as many of these natural athletes as possible. This is understandable in the major leagues, but not in youth baseball. In the big leagues, players' skills have already been developed and the only goal is winning. In youth baseball, when winning is overemphasized, developing skill takes a back seat. The result of stacking a team with talented six-year-olds just so that you can win all the games against the other, less talented six-year-olds is counterproductive. It only serves the parents and the coaches. It does little to help the kids develop as baseball players.

It's okay to be encouraging, but constantly telling kids that they are doing great without correcting their poor technique is just being satisfied with a result that feels good. Feel-good results rarely lead to success. Time passes and you don't get it back, so it's important for kids to develop the discipline to keep up a good effort when they are young. Where young baseball players concentrate their efforts is important because it's a skill-based sport. Playing eighty-five games during the summer on a travel team when you are ten-years-old will not increase your skill level as much as many people think. An alternate approach would be playing half as many games and spending extra time on your personal skill development with correct repetitions. This will lead to sustainable skills as a player grows older. Skills are developed in practice, not in games, but it is hard to convince someone of this when he is more concerned with winning than with training. It is true, however, that playing games allows a player to hone the skills that they have been developing through their practice sessions. The two go hand in hand, and a good balance must be established for complete player development. When you get to high school, it won't matter what team you played for when you were in Little League. Your level of skill, however, *will* matter. Where you placed your efforts when you were young will reveal itself.

The travel team experience can be good or bad. I have seen many young players benefit from playing with, and against, players with abilities similar to their own. They had a passion for baseball and not only did they enjoy playing lots of games during their summer vacation, but they continued to develop their personal skills in the off-season. I believe that these players are the exceptions, however, and others do not fare so well. Some kids may love baseball, but also enjoy doing other things as well while they are young. On some travel teams, so much effort is required in terms of time spent on team practice, and then playing games, that other childhood activities take a back seat, or may not happen at all. The next thing you know, the summer is over and it's time for school again. With this kind of schedule, many kids decide that they no longer like baseball and walk away from it. The efforts of the adults in their lives to turn them into miniature superstars have failed, and there are a lot of devastated fathers whose dream has come to an early end. I know several of them. Unfortunately, this is becoming more common as parents are duped into thinking that being on a certain travel team that plays way too many games, or getting a couple of lessons from a former professional player, will turn their child into a superstar. These things are not bad, but without consistent training on the basics, they are worthless.

If you want misery, focus on outcomes; if you want to have fun and give yourself a chance for success, focus on effort. The truth is that outcomes involve the future and you have no control over the future. Your effort is now and you do have control over that.

Make it your goal to expect kids to do only the things they are capable of doing and see what happens. If you can succeed at this goal, you should expect eventual success from the kids. Make sure that your definition of success is relevant and reasonable. By staying within themselves, kids will be able to have fun and will put forth a winning effort. Their skills will develop and their confidence will grow. By trying too hard, they will make more mental mistakes and thus their effort will be a losing one. When kids try to do more than what they are capable of, it's usually because of pressure that they feel from outcome-oriented parents and coaches.

Play your role as a parent or coach by having realistic expectations of young, inexperienced players.
Whether it's your child's goal to become the best baseball player they can be or to simply play the game as a form of recreation, being consistent with good effort when they are young is important; it is a habit that they will take with them into adulthood.

There are no guarantees that a team will win every game, but individual players can put forth a winning effort every time. By doing this, a player guarantees their own success for the future, whether their team wins or not. Just remember that we don't always get exactly what we want, but good effort is never wasted. Putting forth good effort is such a positive experience that it affects your whole being. Physically and mentally, you will turn yourself into the player and person whom you want to be. A consistent winning effort will lead to sustainable baseball skills and life skills as a player grows older.

Kids do not understand this concept, so it's the adults in their lives who must instill it. Unfortunately, this doesn't always happen. I have seen many youth teams win games with what I would call a losing effort. Coaches who are successful in stacking their teams with the best players in the recreational league will win every time because they have no competition. This is ultimately a losing effort, because the players aren't really required to get the most out of their ability when their team is far superior to the other teams in their league. It's hard to convince a nine-year-old kid to work on his individual skills when he already feels like a superstar because his team always wins. He sees the excitement on the faces of his parents and coaches and, to him, that's success. I was reminded of this again when Bill, a youth coach whose son I teach, told me about a nine-year-old first baseman he encountered during a game. While standing at first base, the little superstar disrespectfully informed Coach Bill that his team had no chance of winning. "We'll catch every ball your players hit; they don't have a chance," he said. On the next pitch, the ball whizzed by him for a double; it was hit by Bill's son Andy.

Lack of respect and arrogance are the partners of failure.

In spite of natural talent, kids who display this behavior are guilty of poor effort and are on the path to failure, not success.

Play your role as a parent and show excitement not only when the team wins, but whenever your child displays winning effort, even if the team loses.

When your child is young, they may be on a team that wins games because the team is stacked with all the talent, or they may be on a team that has no chance of winning. Either way, it's their individual effort that will determine whether or not they will still be playing the game on a competitive level in the future. Effort is always more important than winning because it leads somewhere. Winning doesn't necessarily lead anywhere unless real effort is present. A team that puts out a winning effort always has a chance to win the game and the players will learn to love the *process* instead of the prospect of winning. At every level of competition, when the focus is on the outcome, it can become a distraction, which causes tightness and a tendency to overthink, both of which will slow reflexes.

When young, inexperienced players look at the scoreboard, they only see whether they are winning or losing. If they are ahead, it's easy for them to let down their efforts. They feel that they have already won. If they are behind, it's also easy for them to let down their efforts. They feel that they have lost, as they have not yet learned to play the game one inning at a time, one pitch at a time. They're too concerned with the outcome.

As players become older and more experienced, they can look at the scoreboard and understand strategies that will either help them regain the lead or retain the lead. These players are focused on their effort, which can lead them to a good outcome.

Game Six of the 2011 World Series couldn't have made this point more clearly. The St. Louis Cardinals, facing elimination, were behind 7-5 on the scoreboard in the bottom of the ninth inning with two outs. David Freese, down to his last strike, hit a two-run triple to tie the game. Josh Hamilton then gave the Texas Rangers the lead in the top of the tenth inning with a two-run homer. But the Cardinals answered back in the bottom of the tenth. One strike away from elimination for the second time, and Lance Berkman delivered a single to tie the game, 9-9. The Rangers didn't score in the top of the eleventh and David Freese hit a walk-off homer in the bottom of the eleventh to win the game 10-9 and force a Game Seven. Staying "in the moment" and not worrying about an outcome allowed this to happen.

It should be the goal of every coach and parent to instill in kids the discipline to put forth consistent good effort whether they are ahead or behind on the scoreboard. We can start by putting our own good effort on display, by having the discipline to learn all that we can about our role as a parent or coach. Kids will then be influenced by our good example instead of our poor behavior.

Unfortunately, because of their parents' and coaches' burning desire to see them succeed by winning the game, kids often get the message that winning is the most important thing. A very common scenario in youth baseball is to hear a coach give a motivational talk to his players before the game, telling them that giving it their best effort is the most important thing, and then to watch him throw his arms up in the air and start yelling when the kids make errors or fail to get a clutch hit. Saying one thing but displaying another by your actions never works. Kids will respond to their parents' and coaches' actions, not their words. By being creative with skill-based drills during practice and keeping it fun, coaches and parents can teach kids that determination is what will make them the best player that they can be. If they learn this lesson at a young age, they will not only have more fun and success playing baseball, but they will apply good effort to everything they do in life, giving them a chance for success, whether they become a teacher, carpenter, doctor, nurse, mechanic, or professional baseball player.

Many parents do not have a high level of interest in studying the strategies and techniques of the game of baseball. That's okay. If you are one of them, just sit back and enjoy watching your child play. You may be fortunate enough to have a coach who has dedication and knowledge. Have the patience to support him or her and resist the urge to blame them when things are going bad. Remember that baseball is a difficult sport in which to excel. It takes time and *effort*. It should be looked upon as a journey. One of the ugliest things to witness is an outraged parent in the stands who has very little knowledge but no lack of opinion about what it takes to coach kids who are virtual beginners. The expectations of these parents are way out of balance and they just can't stand it when the kids are unable to play above their current level of ability. They don't understand the concept of mastering the basics before you can expect to win. They want to win now! Make it your goal to not be one of those parents. Make it your goal to be a parent with a winning effort when it comes to how you react as a fan.

If a coach or parent is too concerned about outcomes such as strikeouts, errors, winning or losing, and shows disappointment instead of encouragement when things go bad, it'll cause a young player to try to live up to that person's expectations, which may be unrealistic. They will start to focus on the outcome—because they know that that person will be disappointed—instead of their own effort, and will play tight instead of loose and on automatic. It usually goes downhill from there. Baseball is a very challenging game to play and skills need to be developed. They don't just happen. Have the patience to encourage young players instead of demanding perfection immediately and, over time, you will be amazed at what they can accomplish. It's like creating a beautiful carving. You chip away at it a little at a time. It takes *patience.*

Many times there are outcomes that, on the surface, appear to be a success, but, in fact, only amount to manipulation by adults to feed their own egos or unrealistic expectations. Stacking a team with the most talented six-year-olds just so you can whip all the other teams is one example which was mentioned earlier. I remember when my son was six; it was his first year playing baseball. We were new to the area and didn't know anyone when we signed up at the local rec league. Phillip ended up on one of these stacked teams and they were undefeated during the season. As I sat in the bleachers and watched games, I noticed that there were three or four boys who always played the outfield and never played the infield. In six-year-olds' ball games, the baseball rarely reaches the outfield, especially if the most talented players are in the infield. After a practice, I decided to ask one of the coaches why certain players never played the infield, where all of the action was. His response was, "Which one is your son?" My response was, "Why does that matter?"

I shared with him that my son was the third baseman, but I wasn't talking about my son. I was speaking on behalf of the kids who were designated to the lonely life of a six-year-old in the outfield, where a ball was hardly ever hit. These kids spent most of their time on their knees, playing in the grass.

I still have the newspaper article and photo of the undefeated six-year-olds whose coach allowed them to pound the other teams with scores like 23-1. I am not proud of it, because it doesn't represent real success. It represents a poor effort on the part of a coach who mistreated players on his own team and every other team by ignoring the fact that they were just six-years-old and deserved to be treated fairly. Even the kids who got all the playing time in the infield were given a skewed vision of reality by getting their way every time and never being allowed to experience failure. They were experiencing a feel-good result thanks to their coach, who was successful in making sure that they had no competition by stacking his team. Even worse, perhaps, is the recreational league that allowed it.

My experience in martial arts has shown me what is possible when kids are taught to focus on effort, show respect, and be persistent. These basics, combined with positive reinforcement from their teachers and parents to do their best, will keep the fun in it for kids and produce outcomes that are the real thing. In martial arts, if your child has been awarded a black belt just because you paid the money for the course, they may actually have nothing more than a piece of black cloth. When this happens, the school that has awarded the belt has shown a lack of integrity. If you let yourself believe that your child has really accomplished something, but in fact all that really happened was minimal effort for something that would normally require maximum effort, you are focused on the feel-good outcome. Yes, your child got the belt, but do they really deserve it? If your child is seven or eight-years-old and after two years was awarded a black belt, a little research on your part would reveal that this is unrealistic. My Sensei used to put it like this: "Weak training leads to weak results" —Bob Ozman.

The same can be said when it comes to baseball. When a kid is young, basic skills and attitude are still developing. Being part of a team that prioritizes skill and attitude development over winning games is very important. With this approach, you will be winning for the future. There are many teams in youth sports that have recruited only the players who have displayed early skill development for their age. While there is nothing wrong with putting together the team of your choice, parents should stay aware of how much further skill and attitude development is actually taking place. Are the coaches really knowledgeable teachers of the skills needed to compete at a high level and an older age, or are they satisfied with winning, due to the fact that they have managed to assemble the most talented nine-year-olds? Are you satisfied with being able to say that your child is on the so-called "best travel team," yet he is spending most of his precious time as a young player on the bench, watching others play?

Every year I hear this same story from parents of young players: "We just got back from an out-of-state tournament. We were gone four days and it cost us over one thousand dollars. Our son played two innings the whole tournament, which included five games." Whatever the reason, parents have a choice to seek out another team next time whose goal is becoming competitive through proper training of *every* player over time. Beware that most coaches will say these words, but many do not have the discipline or intentions to follow through with an effort-over-outcome approach once the games begin. On some teams, your child can easily find themselves sitting on the bench as an emergency player, while other players with less ability get most of the playing time due to the fact that they are either the coach's kid or the child of some other influential parent. Remember, your son or daughter will get opportunities in the future based on whether or not they developed their skills when they were young, not because they played on the best team when they were twelve-years-old.

At an early age, games can be won with less-than-excellent player mechanics if the natural ability is there. The problem with this is that the longer a player is allowed to continue with poor mechanics, the harder it will be to correct these mechanics when they get older and the competition is better and more prepared. I have seen many young pitchers experience great success at ten and eleven-years-old just because they threw harder than everyone else. They had a gifted arm, but paid no attention to their throwing motion. They or others have thought, "Why change? It seems to be working." In reality, their success was based on the fact that they could naturally throw fast and the other teams' young, undeveloped hitters just couldn't handle it. Many of them were probably just scared. So instead of paying attention to learning proper mechanics (effort), pitchers are left alone because they are winning games (outcome) for their team of ten-year-olds.

The same can be said of hitting. At an early age, some players display more natural confidence, and the result is that they hit the ball more often. Even if their hitting mechanics have flaws, they are successful because the pitching at a young age is still undeveloped. If these flaws in their swing are not addressed at an early age, they'll be disappointed later, when the pitching becomes more sophisticated. Their muscles will have learned the wrong motion and now it will be difficult to find success against good pitchers with a swing that has worked for them against weak pitching. Also, it can be very difficult, if not impossible, to convince a fifteen or sixteen-year-old player that they need work on their hitting. The wrong motion now feels right to them because that is what their muscles have learned. Now the player's attitude will make the difference. They'll need humility and the ability to show respect to someone who can help them. Once again, with proper effort, it's possible to overcome this obstacle, but it won't happen without the proper attitude. If a player intends to play baseball through his high school years, a coach or parent should not be satisfied with just winning when they are younger. Correct effort and attitude are key.

A Word to Young Ballplayers
Win or lose, attention should be paid to learning the correct mechanics, and to having the proper attitude. Eventually, you will learn to trust that your excellent effort in these areas is what will prepare you to compete as you grow older. If it's your goal to succeed at a high level of baseball, *putting forth good effort means consistent training on the basics.* Not just once in a while, but on a daily basis, with appropriate breaks throughout the year.

When a player gets to high school, no one asks how many wins your team had when you were nine or ten-years-old. No one cares. All that matters now is whether you have trained properly over the years to prepare yourself to compete at a high level. When you were young, were you focused on effort or outcome?

Chapter 4

Staying Positive

A Parent's Role in Helping Kids Stay Positive: stay positive yourself and encourage others to do the same.

Young athletes will be affected by a parent's negative attitude; they will also be affected by a parent's positive attitude. Which one will you have? Your child doesn't have a choice in the matter, but you do. The benefits of staying positive cannot be overstated. This is true in every aspect of life, and is crucial for success in competitive or recreational baseball.

Many parents find it almost impossible to remain positive during a child's sporting event. Lack of patience and the need for instant gratification are two reasons why this happens. Even in recreational baseball, when kids are five and six-years-old, many parents become negative quickly when they think that some other child has received an opportunity that theirs has not. It's an emotional response to something over which they have no control. When a situation is out of your control, how you react as a parent can mean the difference as to whether or not your child will have fun playing the game. If you spend your time trying to manipulate situations over which you have no control, you are likely to act negatively out of frustration because you won't see progress and you can't do anything about it. If you concentrate your efforts on things over which you do have control (helping your own child develop skills), you will see real progress and it's much easier to remain positive. When parents take a positive approach, it's almost impossible for their child to not have fun.

Baseball is a game of reactions. For older, more experienced players, having a positive attitude during the game will allow for quick reaction time and mental discipline, giving them the edge that they need when they need it. If their parents instilled a positive attitude in them at a young age, these older athletes can depend on it. A negative attitude breeds doubt and causes a lack of focus. Parents who are negative will transfer that energy to their child every time. Their child will not be the one making clutch plays or getting that clutch hit when the pressure is on. Being too concerned about outcomes is usually where negativity begins, because it's hard for parents to remain positive when their expectations for their child are not being met. For example, if your child is nine-years-old and you think he should be the shortstop, but the coach's kid gets the position whether he deserves it or not, how are you going to react? There are only two possibilities: you can become negative or you can remain positive. By bad-mouthing the coach behind his back or showing some other display of poor character, you're not helping your child to become a shortstop. A better approach would be learning about the requirements of the position yourself and taking the time to help your child improve his skills.

Staying positive and focusing your efforts on something over which you have control always leads to better things. Complaining about the fact that the coach's son always gets to play shortstop will lead to the same place every time: nowhere. By being negative, you are stifling your child's efforts while you stroke your own ego. By staying positive, you will remain on the path of skill development, allowing your child's efforts to grow, and you will be making progress toward helping your child become a shortstop. Think of it this way: your child is not always going to be a nine-year-old baseball player. As he grows older, his skills are going to have to improve anyway if he expects to compete at higher levels of play, so why not focus on your child's effort and personal development instead of whether or not the coach is being fair? Through this positive process, you may even realize that your child is better suited for a position other than shortstop. This is a winning way.

A positive approach creates awareness; a negative approach creates mindlessness.

Understanding what you can control and what you can't is the first step in gaining a positive attitude. Blaming the umpire is the most popular excuse parents come up with when their child is struggling, but blaming the coach is a close second. All it takes is one negative parent to start the complaining and soon everyone jumps on the bandwagon.

A player must strive to be positive the whole game, not just when the team is ahead in the score. Negative thinking during competition always affects performance. If a player's thinking becomes negative, they will play tight and not be as quick as they need to be on defense. Their hitting will also suffer because their mind won't let go of the last time at bat, when the umpire caused them to strike out. If they think that they can wait to have a positive attitude, by waiting until something positive happens, they are approaching the game backwards and they will need a lot of luck. Planning on being lucky is a poor approach.

You must think positively to obtain positive results. For some, this is harder than learning a physical skill. Without proper instruction and influence, many young players will go through this cycle of positive, negative, positive, negative throughout the game, basically letting the game play them. If they see that the pitcher is the other team's ace, for example, many players are defeated before they get in the batter's box. A

negative thought enters their mind; they see themselves striking out and then, predictably, it happens. (They also have an
excuse: "The pitcher is too good for me.") After they have a
bad at-bat (you can strike out and still have a good at-bat),
they take their negative experience with them on defense.
Now, they are more likely to make errors. You've got nothing
to lose by staying positive; you've got everything to lose by being negative. By staying positive, at least you give yourself a
chance against a dominant pitcher and, instead of making excuses for yourself you will respect his ability. You might even
be inspired to strive for that level of excellence yourself. Showing respect is positive. Making excuses is negative.

A positive attitude is contagious, but so is a negative attitude. In fact, a negative attitude can be just as effective, when
it comes to how it affects the team, as a positive one. This is
because many people find it much easier to latch on to a negative attitude; therefore, it happens more often. For some parents who don't get their way, having a negative attitude gives
them a feeling of power and a sense of superiority. While this
may make them feel good for a little while, it does nothing to
help their child have fun and become a better baseball player.
Oddly, whether they know it or not, these parents have come
to trust that a negative attitude will produce the expected results (failure) and they are right. It feels good to be right. Now,
when failure happens, they have an "I told you so" attitude and
will find someone to blame.

Negative people expect failure; positive people expect success.

A positive attitude is a character trait that is missing at many
youth sporting events. Immediate gratification is the culprit.
When instant results are not achieved, many parents figure
that there must be a reason, something other than their child's
lack of effort, lack of ability, poor attitude, or lack of training.
Blaming the coach is convenient, but is usually not the answer.
Parents with a need to see instant results, who do not understand the process of developing skills, will blame someone else
every time. It's impossible for them to have a positive attitude,
because that means giving up control or having to admit that

their child needs help. Having a positive attitude suggests being patient, respectful, and happy for someone else's success, and it entails having the ability to accept criticism. A negative attitude is just the opposite. Having a positive attitude is so difficult for many people because it does not guarantee instant success. It only suggests eventual success.

Depending on the circumstances, "eventual" could mean during this game or the next season, which is not quick enough for many.

It's easy to understand why people lack patience when they know very little about the game of baseball, but it's hard to understand an adult's apparent lack of concern about negative behavior in the presence of kids. Many times a negative attitude at a kid's baseball game starts in the stands from certain parents who expect instant results. A negative attitude will surely produce instant results: negative results. It can cause players to give up. Just as we can't expect kids to play like adults, we also can't expect them to ignore the negative comments coming from the stands, especially the ones from their parents.

These negative comments are fueled by the need for instant gratification.

While staying positive is crucial for success, it doesn't guarantee success. There are many other things to consider, such as a player's ability, individual effort, coaching expertise, parent support, and the makeup of the other team as well, as it relates to having success. Some things you have control over, and some things you do not. If we focus on the things over which we have control, we can expect eventual success. When parents do not understand this truth, "eventual" is not a word that they want to hear when it comes to their child's baseball experience. Although they would never admit it, these unenlightened parents want to hear the word "immediate."

During a baseball game, many things will happen over which we have no control. Striking out, the sun in your eyes, bad calls by the umpire, poor field conditions, and a couple of players who didn't show up are just a few examples. This is when we find out who has developed a positive attitude and who has not. For those who have not, it probably won't happen today. For some, it may never happen unless they first develop humility. Once the bad habit of a negative attitude has taken hold, it will take some time to turn it around.

Just like overcoming bad habits with a physical skill such as hitting, pitching, and fielding, it takes time to correct a negative attitude that has become a part of your character. Also, it must be remembered, there are so many things that can go wrong in a ball game, that sometimes even a positive attitude will not give you the result that you want. But a negative attitude will almost always seal your fate with failure, unless you get lucky.

Once again, depending on luck is a poor approach. Parents and coaches are the ones the kids will mimic when it comes to attitude. If a coach or a parent is negative, how do you think a kid will react? They are supposed to learn from us and, believe me, they will.

Play your role as a parent by showing your kids, by example, that a positive attitude is what will allow you to see through the negative, and be able to notice all the good that is happening around you.

Staying Positive During Competition

I decided one year to organize a baseball team based out of my school, Chuck's Gym, where I teach martial arts and baseball skills. The goal was to develop a team in which everyone trained together and parents agreed on the training philosophy when it came to kids and baseball. The team would develop skill and continuity over a period of years, much like a martial arts program.

We started the program with a few interested families in September, to prepare for the spring season. I had already been giving hitting lessons to their kids and had coached some of them during the fall recreational league. Everyone was very pleased with their sons' improvement and was very interested when I mentioned starting a team with their nine-year-old players. We eventually found a total of eleven families who expressed interest in our program. Everyone saw the need for a well-balanced, *realistic* approach for developing a competitive baseball team when starting with nine-year-old players. We discussed the real possibility of not winning many games during the first year in the travel league. Many of the other teams had been together for three years already and were very organized because of it. We all knew that they would be hard to beat.

We all agreed that we had our work cut out for us and that it would take time and effort to become competitive as a team. As it turns out, all the kids hit the ball very well because of the instruction and repetitions they were getting in the off-season. The problem was defense. At the first parent meeting, the coaches discussed and stressed the need for repetitions for throwing and catching, in addition to the hitting instruction. We went over the basic techniques for throwing and catching with the parents to make sure that their kids were repeating the motions correctly. Basically, parents just playing catch; hitting ground balls and fly balls to their kids on a regular basis would have done it. It was very apparent in the first few practices of the season, however, that this goal was not accomplished and, when the scheduled games began, our team was not making routine plays on defense and the other more experienced teams were. It did not matter how well we hit because our throwing and catching skills were not developed nearly as well as the other teams'. We were not on a level playing field because the effort was not put forth to increase catching and throwing skills in the preceding months.

After losing many games, some parents decided that it was the coaches' fault for not being able to "win the close ones." Instead of accepting responsibility for not helping their kids develop skill by playing catch with them on a regular basis, they pretended that their kids were trained athletes and disrespected the three very experienced coaches by blaming them for the team's losses. Everything that we had talked about at the parent meeting at the beginning of the season was forgotten when some parents took a negative attitude toward losing, and emotions and lack of perspective took over. What many parents fail to realize is that, at this young age, the kids are *all* beginners and the path to excellence is long. *Talent alone will not guarantee success.* Every one of the players on that team of nine-year-olds will eventually have to face their weaknesses and it will be those who have adopted a positive attitude that will overcome them. By staying positive, parents can help their kids learn to not blame others and come to understand that "you cannot skip the basics and go right to the winning."

Although coaches are sometimes blamed in the recreational leagues as well, there is a fundamental difference between these leagues and the travel leagues. In the recreational league, it is common to see *both* teams not making the routine plays. Because they are on a similar level, no one dominates, and the kids have fun.

In his book, *Coaching Youth Baseball the Ripken Way*, Cal Ripken, Jr. says that "The most successful teams are the ones that play catch the best." At the youth level, this is especially true, because it's very discouraging when your team manages to score six or seven runs and then gives them all back on defense because of the inability to catch routine fly balls and ground balls. When your opponent makes all of the routine plays, they are only giving you three outs. When *your* team does not make the routine plays, you are giving your opponent as many outs as your poor defense will allow. If your team makes four errors, for example, you just gave the other team seven outs. If you consistently do this, how can you expect to win?

When you put a team in the travel leagues and are unprepared, such as this team of nine-year-olds was, you will find it hard to win games, and even harder to have fun. You will not be on the same skill level as other teams and, consequently, you will not be competitive. When your team is not competitive, certain parents who have been hiding their negative attitude will now become very vocal and it's hard, if not impossible, to teach skills, because the team becomes dysfunctional.

The positive attitude that everyone started out with is replaced with doubt, blaming, and negativity. If your team finds itself in this unenviable position, staying positive and focusing on effort is *crucial* for the sake of your child. If a team is fortunate enough to have parents who live by positive standards, things will go well and the kids will learn and have fun in spite of not winning many games. Success can still happen in the way of skill development and everyone will have learned this valuable lesson for the future: *If you want success, you prepare for success.* Unfortunately, it only takes one or two "outcome-oriented" parents to ruin it for everyone. They just have to win! Instead of staying positive and realizing what skills their kids need to work on, these disruptive parents start blaming coaches, and are very intolerant of other players on the team whom *they* feel are not as talented as their kids. These parents also feel inclined to share their misguided beliefs with others in the stands for the rest of the season. This divides the team and takes the focus off of just enjoying watching the kids play baseball. A negative attitude and a lack of perspective are like cancer to a team. If it is not detected early and dealt with effectively, it will spread to others as the seed of doubt is planted. Every parent's emotions can get the best of them. Because we care so much for our kids, no one is exempt. This is why staying positive during competition is so important to the success of a team. *It is an antidote for failure.*

First Parent Meeting
Developing a program where we as coaches and parents are working together for the betterment of our young players, not only in baseball, but in life, should be a high priority. I am sure that every parent would admit that, if an important meeting were called at their workplace, it would be of a high priority and they would make every conceivable effort to be there. Yet many times only one parent shows up at the parent meeting for the baseball team. When the season starts, you see both parents at the games. One is informed; one is uninformed because they didn't come to the parent meeting. This would be like not showing up at a company meeting where important information is being presented about some new product or the company's future, and you think you can "just wing it," so you don't go. I think you would agree that not showing up would be a poor choice.

Every year there are those who choose not to come to the first parent meeting. They come up with this excuse: "Baseball is my spouse's passion; I really don't know anything about it, so they can handle it." To those folks I would say, "Although I have a love for the game, coaching baseball isn't my passion, but teaching kids valuable life lessons through the game of baseball and keeping it fun is." Your kids are your passion, not baseball. For parents, these meetings should be more about learning your role as a parent than learning about baseball itself. If parents become proficient at playing their role in a positive way, their kids will benefit. Especially when kids are young, parents are every bit a part of the team as the players and coaches. If parents do not play their role in a positive way, it will have a negative effect on the whole season.

When the season begins, both parents will be high on emotion, because it's their child out there on the field. The informed parent has a better chance of playing their role correctly by staying positive, because good information was presented at the parent meeting and they were listening. They will have gained perspective. The uninformed parent is usually functioning on 100% emotion, and this is where problems start. They will believe what their emotions tell them and react accordingly, usually to the detriment of the team, their own child, and themselves. Disrespecting umpires, coaches, other players, and embarrassing their own child by coaching from the stands are very common traits of the uninformed parent. They have a misguided sense that their emotions are always correct. This is a pretty common situation, so it's very beneficial if both parents make it to the parent meeting with an open mind because a lot of good information is presented at these meetings. Whether the volunteer coaches are experienced or not, most likely their intentions are good and this is where adopting a positive attitude for the season is born. For many, it dies once the competition begins because they are putting too much importance on outcome and when their expectations are not realized, their emotions take over and their attitude becomes negative.

If you do not control your emotions, your emotions will control you.

If we approach youth baseball with the goal of understanding our role as parents, we will take advantage of all the opportunities to teach life lessons and strive to become more informed and aware for our kid's sake. We will be showing interest in their interests and that can go a long way in helping them develop as a player and as a person. It also makes it easier for us to stay positive when games begin, because now we will view success in a different way. In this respect, baseball is a real gift. The kids will have fun because we as adults have a good perspective, and they will get the most out of their baseball experience whether they win or lose the game. If we think of kids as miniature professionals, we are likely to focus more on outcomes instead of effort, and things can become negative quickly if the team isn't winning.

In his book *Head Games*, Walter Herbison says: "Positive thoughts result in positive actions." He calls it *Head Game One*. He goes on to ask: How do we make use of *Head Game One*? For starters, make a choice. Choose to be positive.

Chapter 5

Patience

A Parent's Patient Role in Their Child's Baseball Journey: allow your child to have fun while taking the necessary steps to develop skill.

Slowing down their own child's progress is a consequence that many parents had not counted on when they were orchestrating their child's rise to baseball stardom.

There are always consequences for a lack of patience.

By making it about themselves instead of their child, parents are not aware of their child's needs. They are only aware of their own needs. Since they are not the ones who need to develop the skill necessary to perform the difficult tasks associated with baseball, many parents do not fully understand and respect the challenges that kids face.

Baseball pioneer and executive Branch Rickey said that "baseball is a game of inches." What he meant was that an inch or two can mean the difference between success and failure in many ways throughout the game. Relatively speaking, this is true for a six-year-old player, as well as for a major-league player. One of the things that makes baseball such a great sport is the fact that challenges are presented every step of the way at every level of play. Because it's challenging, patience is required for a desirable outcome, just as in all aspects of our lives. Unfortunately, adults lacking patience with kids is very common at youth baseball fields across this country. It's unbelievable to watch a baseball game with seven-year-old players whose parents and coaches expect them to have the physical and mental maturity of much older and more experienced players, an impossible task that takes the fun out of baseball for these young players.

Are you having any success with being patient while your child struggles with this "game of inches" as it applies to the difficult tasks of hitting, pitching, throwing, and catching a baseball? If not, it's your child who will need an unusual amount of patience in order to deal with your unrealistic expectations. All of these skills require accuracy to achieve consistent good results. The best way for a player to develop accuracy is by mastering the basics, which takes time. There's no doubt that, when kids are young, it's very challenging for parents and coaches to teach basics while keeping it fun. The kids have very little patience, but this only means that they're normal. When parents and coaches have very little patience, what does that mean?

When parents place faith in shortcuts and quick fixes instead of proper training, their child's skills remained undeveloped, time passes, and a huge learning opportunity has been missed. A lack of patience has ended many kids' baseball dreams because the necessary process of skill development was not allowed to happen. When a player's skill is not being developed, it's only a matter of time until frustration develops and *dominates* their baseball experience, because they can't compete with other players who have taken the time to develop their skills.

It's understandable when a kid is impatient, because they have very little experience upon which to draw. What doesn't make sense is for parents and coaches to seek instant results just to satisfy their own egos and expectations. "It's for the kids" is a phrase often heard at parent meetings and in casual conversation at youth ball parks, yet expecting too much from kids is what you often witness from these parents once the game starts, because they make it about themselves by wanting things to happen too soon. Speaking on behalf of the kids, not only should we have respect for the difficulty of the game of baseball, but, when the competition begins, we should remember their young age. It is the parents' and coaches' *responsibility* to have patience when teaching basics and to ultimately pass that trait on to the young players. If not, many young players will quit or grow up with the same bad habit of being selfishly impatient.

A key component to being successful at having patience is an understanding of how it applies to, or is relative to, any given event. Telling your child that it's time to leave for school, or asking them to do a chore and finding that they ignore you, are different from expecting them to accomplish something very difficult (like hitting a baseball) without letting them take the necessary steps to develop the skill required to achieve it. If you find yourself rushing your child's development as a skilled baseball player, maybe your expectations are too high and you are seeking immediate results.

When kids are young, some parents are very manipulative and play politics with coaches to give their kids an advantage over others. It's a good idea to resist this desperate behavior because it will no longer work at higher levels of play. It also sends the wrong message to kids, which is that when things aren't going fast enough or going your way, you will resort to anything to get what you want. Remember this: The level of difficulty of the skill, compared with your child's natural ability, interest and desire, should be your guide to how much patience you will need to help them have fun and succeed. For example, if the goal is to be a successful player on a very advanced competitive team, a persistent approach to skill development will be required at an early age. *It takes time to develop*

Training to Avoid Injury

Kids need to train on the proper footwork and hand placement before you put them in the outfield with a baseball coming at them at high speed. Skipping this step can lead to unpleasant consequences. Practicing with sponge rubber balls or tennis balls to avoid injury is a good idea for young players. Teach them to catch the ball with both hands above and in front of the head and look the ball into the glove. Start by tossing balls from a short distance. When you are confident that they understand and can execute the technique, they are ready for longer fly balls. This can take some time, but it is the patient approach and it will help avoid injury. Be creative with younger players by turning your drills into a game to keep them interested.

skill. As they grow older, if their passion for baseball also grows, you and your child may discuss expectations for their future in baseball. If they expect to play in college, especially at a high level, developing skill and athleticism is Goal Number One.

Even in recreational baseball, where the makeup of teams is more diverse in terms of players' skills, some kids will struggle more than others because of lack of ability and attention span. They still deserve patience from parents and coaches. I remember a young coach asking me for advice about his team of five and six-year-olds. He said, "Some of the kids can do the drills we teach them and some are just not close." He went on to describe how hard it was to keep their attention: "When they're on defense, they are either looking off into space or playing in the dirt." I explained to him that, at this young age, not paying attention and playing in the dirt is more normal than being focused and productive. The ones who are focused and productive at this age are the unusual ones. Just like it takes a five or six-year-old kid time to develop in these areas, it takes time for an inexperienced coach to develop the necessary knowledge to teach all of them, whether they have natural ability or not. My only advice to him was: keep learning and *have patience.*

Having patience is easier said than done. You need to work at it and be patient with yourself. Don't give up and start saying things like "I just don't have patience with kids," thinking that this is some sort of license to yell at, or expect too much from kids who are just trying to have fun. What if a kid were to say, "I just don't have patience with adults," and then do whatever they want when they don't get their way. I suppose that we would call that a lack of respect.

During my thirty-plus years of teaching martial arts and baseball, I have realized that achieving *excellence* in these disciplines will require as much patience as you can muster. Just becoming average can be challenging. They are both very precise and skill-oriented activities and need to be looked upon as journeys. Basics need to be mastered before you can expect kids to execute advanced techniques.

When coaches challenge kids with advanced drills before they are ready, not only are they setting them up for failure, but injuries can happen. Every year you hear about kids getting hit in the face from a fly ball. For a seven-year-old kid, catching a long fly ball is an advanced skill. Inexperienced coaches often send their young players to the outfield and hit fly balls to them without first teaching proper catching technique. It's a mistake to think that every kid can catch a fly ball without first showing them the correct and safe way to do it. It sounds easy, but for some kids, especially young ones, catching a baseball does not come naturally. What comes naturally is fear of being hit in the face by the baseball. If coaches and parents have not taken the time to show them how to do it, kids will have no confidence in their ability to catch the ball and are more likely to be hit by the ball.

Teaching proper technique, to the point where it is a natural reaction, takes time and perseverance.

If you are a volunteer coach and your only definition of success is winning games, there is no way that you will have the patience to teach kids proper fundamentals, because skill development takes too long. You will use the naturally talented players and just leave kids who can't perform on the bench, or try to hide them on the field where you think no balls will be hit (usually right field in youth baseball), instead of taking the time to help them. Outcome-oriented coaches, whose priority is winning games, often overlook skill development, even for the naturally gifted players. It's easy to get caught up in the glory of winning all the games with a talented team of twelve-year-olds, forgetting that these kids are also virtual beginners on their journey toward excellence. Inexperienced coaches may not see the flaws in a young player's technique because, at their current age, the flaws are less noticeable; all the players have them. If they continue to play, the flaws will become more noticeable because they will eventually be playing against players who took the time to develop their skills. Chances are that these advanced players had coaches and parents who took the time to teach skills whether the team was winning or losing. The outcome of the game was secondary; skill development was the top priority. Choose to be one of those coaches or parents.

When parents and coaches try to rush the process, it's difficult for skill development to happen for a young player, because these unenlightened adults are not performing their role correctly. They expect kids to be able to *just do it,* and if they can't, parents and coaches who lack patience do not take the time to show kids the correct technique. One reason for this may be that the parents and coaches do not know the correct technique themselves. Coaches especially need to be diligent in learning basics and the correct way to teach them to young kids. If this goal is accomplished, kids will learn to be persistent in their own training because the techniques will make sense.

Perform your role as a parent or coach by taking the time to learn the basics and to teach them, and by having the patience to let your kids master them before moving on to more advanced techniques.

There is another situation in which an impatient parent affects their kids in a negative way, and that is the case of the overbearing parent. These arrogant parents are going to make sure skill development happens and it can't happen soon enough for them. Skill development happens all right, but it usually happens at the expense of the young player's enjoyment. It becomes a job for them. This is often the case for naturally talented kids whose eager parents see their child's natural ability for more than it really is. When these parents get too ambitious with the progress of their talented young player, they are likely to make their child overdose on baseball, with a schedule of games that resembles something from the major leagues. This impractical approach usually has the effect of depriving kids of other crucial aspects of their childhood. Family vacations, church camps, and many other nurturing activities take a back seat to baseball tournaments all summer long, until it is time for school to begin again. Playing lots of games is important for experience, but a realistic balance with other normal childhood activities must be achieved for the sake of the young player. Playing too many games has the effect of burning kids out on the game of baseball. Playing a reasonable amount of games, combined with individual practice, is crucial for skill development and has the effect of building confidence, developing patience, and increasing interest in the game of baseball. This equation is not the same for everyone, so parents should pay attention to their own child's level of interest.

Most kids want to be kids in every sense of the word, not just baseball kids. Stay aware of how much your child has learned each step of the way through the process; you will then see the progress. Help them take the next step on the journey instead of looking for shortcuts. Many times, people who become impatient get lost while taking so-called "shortcuts." The best shortcut is to stay on the path, building on what you have already learned. By doing this, skill will develop, confidence will grow, and you will be moving forward toward your goal; you will be succeeding. This truth applies to both parents and kids, but the parents have to understand it first. When parents are patient, success will be achieved because kids will get the most out of their ability over time instead of getting burnt out because their parents want too much too soon. When kids feel like they are achieving success, they will be having fun.

Be as patient with your own child as you are with other kids. When you start losing patience, maybe it's time to re-examine your goals and expectations for your child. Are yours out of balance with theirs? Maybe re-evaluate your child's interest level for the activity as it relates to the difficulty and time required to accomplish the goal. Do they just want the benefits that reaching the goal will offer, or do they value the experience of the journey to get there? If your own behavior reflects a desire for instant results, it will be easy for your child to have that exact same attitude.

Play your role as a parent by not losing patience because of your own need for instant gratification through immediate results.

Many people who have found great success will tell you that it was the journey that was the fun part; the discovery along the way, meeting and working with people like themselves who have similar goals; the excitement and hunger for success and the sacrifices that were made to achieve it. With this approach, slowly but surely, confidence is gained so that when you finally reach the end of your journey you are prepared to deal with new challenges that await you as you move forward. By enjoying the process, living your life, and not being obsessed with results, you will stay the course and your ultimate success will be the result of your excellent journey. You will be experienced. For a young baseball player, success is achieved along the way by learning how to overcome the obstacles that confront them on the journey; it does not necessarily mean winning the Little League World Series. By putting forth the kind of persistent effort that it takes to get the most out of their ability, they are learning how to succeed in life by being patient and determined. This is a winning way.

Along with baseball skills, there are many life lessons that we can and should teach young ballplayers. We can do this by helping them establish realistic short and long-term goals, which will allow them to experience the path to excellence on their own terms, not their parents'. Having short-term goals will also help parents establish a patient approach to their child's baseball experience as their child builds on their success with each stage of the process. Developing skills one step at a time will take the pressure off of kids so that they will be willing to try new things, willing to take a few risks because they know that the adults around them are patient and supportive. Have the tolerance to let kids experience a little failure, and be ready to teach them how to deal with it. If you, as a parent or coach, can display patience on a consistent basis, kids will also learn to be patient. Once you have developed patience, it can be there for you to use whenever and wherever you need it.

When patience is not present in youth sports, it usually means one thing: the parents and coaches want results too soon! In this instant-gratification society, young people are taught to be impatient from the word "go." As soon as they realize that they can get something by whining and their parents don't have the backbone to say "no," kids are learning to be impatient and may one day pass that undesirable trait on to their own children. When parents continually make excuses for their kids in youth sports or add too much pressure because they want them to succeed right away without going through all of the effort, ultimate success may elude them, all because of a lack of patience.

What is patience and why don't we have it? It can be hard to explain when we are talking about the big picture, that is to say, our basic personality. In youth sports, many people do not show patience when it comes to the development of their young athletes and the unfortunate results are easy to see. Blaming others, giving up, and making excuses are just a few. There can be many reasons why parents lack patience, but here is a common one: They may be paying too much attention to another player who is enjoying some success for one reason or another. They probably do not understand why that player is experiencing success. They just know that that they want the same or better for their kid. Now there is a sense of urgency. How do we get there quickly? Maybe a new "state of the art" bat? Maybe a few hitting lessons with a former pro ball player who lives in the area? Maybe some of his magic will rub off on my kid if we get a "tune-up" right before tryouts? All of these things are okay, but will not guarantee the desired results. What these people really want is instant results (immediate gratification). Deep down, they cannot bear to have to wait while someone else's kid is soaking up the spotlight. They lose patience. I have seen many examples in which parents refuse to see the situation for what it *really* is—their kid is not prepared for the task at hand, and for some reason, others already are.

I remember one incident when I was coaching a team of eight and nine-year-olds. One of the more talented players on the team, Joey, would react by "tearing up" when he experienced failure during the game. Maybe it was a strikeout, or an error, or struggling as a pitcher. Finally, after a strikeout in our fifth game of the season, Joey walked back to the dugout with his head down and tears in his eyes. His dad, who was helping out as an assistant coach, grabbed him by the shoulders and pulled him aside and, in a stern voice, informed him that "There's no crying in baseball!" Joey was eight-years-old at the time. He would never admit it, but Joey's father was embarrassed that Joey did not have the maturity to just "suck it up" like some of the other players. He made the situation about himself, instead of realizing that Joey, at only eight-years-old, hadn't quite matured enough to be able to just let it go. Maybe Joey felt pressure to succeed because of his dad's lack of patience, instead of being able to develop and grow at a normal pace. Some parents and coaches learn from these situations; others do not. When they do not, it's the kid who suffers.

Patience is the ability to be at peace with a situation as it develops. Not living in the past, not living in the future, but living in the present moment. To be patient, you need an understanding that you cannot control an outcome. You can only control your attitude about the situation and encourage someone else, like your child, to do the same.

So how do you develop patience? This can take some soul-searching. Until you finally see the consequences of your lack of patience, you probably won't do anything to change. You don't see it as your problem because of your lack of knowledge and understanding about a number of other issues. When you finally admit to yourself that it might be your own lack of patience with your child's current rate of development that is actually slowing him down even more, things will change. You will then have humility and a newfound awareness of what it takes to become a patient person, and you will see the amazing benefits that come with it. Your child is the one who will benefit most. When you develop patience, you will no longer be robbing your child of the joy of competition. If you ever want to witness a lack of patience for yourself, just go to any youth baseball game. You will see and hear lack of patience in real time. "Throw strikes!" is what most young pitchers hear from parents and inexperienced coaches when they are struggling to get the ball over the plate. All that this accomplishes is putting more pressure on a kid who already might feel like he is letting everyone down. It never helps him. He has been trying to throw strikes. What he *needs* is some useful information from a coach who has taken the time to learn a little bit about pitching. If all you can come up with is "Throw strikes!" when your pitcher is struggling, you don't know much about pitching and should at least buy a book on the subject.

Another often-heard phrase at youth ball games is "You gotta have that one!" This happens when a young player doesn't make a play on defense. If a player isn't paying attention, there may be some truth in that statement. But often a ball is just out of reach or takes a bad hop and people just start yelling and expecting a player to make a play that was actually a base hit. It was not a routine play; the young player did all that he could do, and was yelled at. This is not helpful and you are not playing your role as a parent very well if you do it. What the player really needed in this instance was praise for his great effort. Impatient people who know very little about the game have a tendency to yell at kids who are just trying to do their best.

Even if you know nothing about baseball, you can perform your role as a parent or coach very well by adopting the rule that you will have the patience to not yell at kids who are just doing their best.

As a parent or coach, you can improve your level of patience by increasing your knowledge of the game. This takes time and effort on your part, but is well worth it for your child's or team's sake. The more you learn, the more respect you will gain for the physical and mental skills needed to play the game. Put yourself in your kid's shoes. Could you, as an adult, do what you are asking a nine-year-old kid to do, for example? Try it sometime; see if *you* can "throw strikes" or "hit the baseball." Just because your kid is nine-years-old, it doesn't mean that he can automatically do these things. In fact, it's pretty much a guarantee that, without some proper instruction, he can't, just like you can't.

When you develop patience for the "process," you will begin to see your child's *effort* instead of his failures. Being a patient person will also allow you to have more appropriate responses to situations on and off the field. Because of this enlightenment, you will be playing your role as a parent very well. Your child will become a better ballplayer because of it.

Sean, a seven-year-old student of mine, has a very impatient father. Sean is quite talented, but already, at seven, quite frustrated. His father is the source of that frustration. During the first six lessons, we discussed the possibility that travel teams would be interested in Sean because of his natural ability. Sean's father asked my opinion about these very competitive teams and I recommended against them in favor of individual training on skill development in addition to playing at his local recreational league. He didn't take my advice and has Sean playing on both teams. Now, seven-year-old Sean has two baseball coaches, a private hitting instructor, and an impatient father. This can be confusing to an adult, let alone a seven-year-old. Sean has gone from being an excellent, easy-to-teach student, to someone who is almost impossible to teach because he has so many expectations placed on him by so many adults. He is confused about to whom he should listen, and from my experience, kids who are getting mixed signals from too many adults are not having fun. It is said that training can be frustrating, confusing, and time-consuming. It takes patience, perseverance, and endurance. In this case, Sean's father does not have the patience to endure the perseverance that it takes to develop skill. His attitude reflects his desire for Sean to play like an experienced athlete right now, forgetting that he is only seven-years-old.

Sean eventually quit the travel team, and remained on his recreational team. As it turns out, the travel team experience only frustrated Sean, mainly because of the coach's lack of knowledge about teaching skills to seven-year-old kids. On one occasion, Sean was hit in the face by a long fly ball. The impatient coach put the kids in the outfield so that they could practice catching fly balls, *before he taught them how to catch fly balls.* I watched a game one evening in which Sean was playing first base for his recreational team. Two pop-ups were hit near him and he watched both of them fall to the ground before picking up the baseball. Because of his bad experience of being hit in the face by the ball, he is now more afraid than ever. He was probably afraid before he got hit in the face as well, because down deep he knew that no one had taken the time to show him the proper technique to catch the long fly ball safely. He had no confidence that he could do it. The consequence for lack of patience on the part of his coach and his father is Sean getting hit in the face by a very hard baseball. Now, Sean has to overcome fear. This is not easy to do and it will slow down his progress in developing skill as a baseball player. This phrase sums up the approach Sean's father took toward his son's training: *The faster you want something to happen, the longer it takes.*

In many cases, young players have not developed their mental and physical skills to the level of expectations of their parents. Until balance is established in this parent/child dynamic, forward progress will be slow, or will not happen at all.

Some parents figure this out early on; others do not. For those who do understand, I say "good for you." You will now have realistic expectations based on whatever ability and interest your child has in baseball. You will be able to witness your child's joy because you have the wisdom and *patience* to play your role in your child's journey.

Chapter 6

Humility

A Parent's Role in Teaching Humility to Kids: through your own actions, demonstrate that humility starts by showing respect to others.

"I know."

These two words are often spoken by those who don't know, but whose egos deny this lack of knowledge. Because of these two words, people are likely to repeat the same wrong thing over and over, hoping for a different result, and the learning process will be slow or will not happen at all. In order to learn, you must open your mind with a willingness to accept what a more knowledgeable person has to offer, letting go of your self-assertive nature and having respect, so that new information has a chance to grow in you. I understand; this is not easy to do.

When humility is absent from a person's character, the mind is not open to learning.

Parents who lack humility will not be effective in learning their role and will become a roadblock in their child's baseball journey. They will only see the end result, but not the steps to get there. Kids who have "know-it-all" parents often mimic this behavior themselves, even as young as six-years-old. When this happens, it's a detour in the learning process because until they learn to be humble, players of all ages will likely be stacking the cards against themselves by practicing incorrect techniques or not practicing at all.

The ancient Greek philosopher Epictetus puts it this way: "It is impossible for anyone to begin to learn that which he thinks he already knows."

Arrogant parents and coaches who refuse to accept advice from others more experienced than themselves will see the results of this egotistical behavior when their kids get older. Time will pass and the full potential of these unfortunate kids will not be realized because the adults in their lives lacked humility in playing their role. Those players who, when they were young, had parents and coaches with more humble attitudes, will have gotten the most out of their ability because while others were *pretending*, they and their parents and coaches were *learning*.

Being humble allows you to have an understanding that arrogant people lack: that things that are difficult take time to develop, sometimes many years. By reflecting on the progress that your child has already made in their life, whether it's in baseball, music, or rock climbing, you will develop trust for the process of skill development and learn to recognize the many steps that have been taken so far and still need to be taken to continue on the path. As you and your child go forward with their training, it's important to remain humble and open to learning, because if you forget where you came from, you may start thinking that your child was just a genius all along. When this happens, things will change for the worse.

Parents who lack humility also lack respect for the process of developing oneself to their full potential. They think that their child is the best and that practice is for the weak.

Ultimately, this blind approach leads to failure, because the passing of time has a way of revealing the truth. Baseball skills are one of those things that take time to develop and there are no shortcuts.

Not taking the shortcut is the shortcut.

When parents take an arrogant approach to training, their kids will follow suit. The difference, however, is that parents tend to be arrogant because their egos can't stand when their kid doesn't get what they want or some other kid gets something that their child did not. When kids see their parents act like this, they often interpret it to mean that by acting arrogantly, we get what we want. They think that it leads to becoming a better ballplayer.

What a mistake!

If you do not take the time required to develop your skills for the level of play you desire, you will eventually fail, even if you are arrogant.

There are certain things that we take for granted because we were expected or required to do them as we were growing up. We don't even realize what we are learning. When I was young, my older brothers and I were required to help out on the family farm. We learned to safely run large farm machinery at a very early age. We didn't think anything about it. All of the farm kids did the same. At school, we became proficient at many things over a period of years. Even if we didn't want to do the farm work or schoolwork, we had to and we learned a lot in spite of ourselves. We had no choice in the matter.

In these cases, such as school and farm work, we didn't need humility as much as we needed respect. *By having respect we developed humility.* They go hand in hand. Because of our unique experiences growing up, where respect and humility were required (or there would be consequences), we became proficient at many things of which we were not even aware. Although I didn't get to play as much baseball as I would have liked, the lessons that our parents taught us on the family farm about putting forth good effort with humility and respect have become valuable tools that I use in all aspects of my life, including teaching kids martial arts and baseball.

When it comes time for us to help our kids pursue their interests, such as baseball, it's not *required* that they do anything; they must want to do it. First of all, kids should be having fun playing baseball or they will not want to do it, even though you may be able to talk them into it. Remember, playing baseball is not a job. Playing baseball is, however, a great way to teach the life lessons required in holding down a job later in life. Players who lack respect and humility will not be putting forth a good effort and opportunities will pass them by, in baseball and in life. It is the responsibility of coaches and parents to instill discipline and respect with the outcome being humility. Whether or not kids will be able to reach their full potential in life will largely depend on their attitude. Will it be one of humility, or arrogance and pride? There are usually negative consequences for arrogance and pride.

Contrary to popular belief, humility is a sign of strength, not of weakness.

If your child is one of the more talented players on your team or league, they are likely to be receiving praise much of the time for their role as the superstar. If your own response is one of arrogance and pride, you will not be helping your child on their baseball journey. If your child adopts this same attitude and continues on this path of arrogance, it's a weakness which usually catches up with them at some point, and the outcome is not what they expected. The day comes when the baseball journey is over and the real-life journey begins. By lacking humility, not only will these players fail to get the most out of their physical ability, but many of the life lessons that are being taught along the way will be missed.

Over the many years I have coached and taught kids, I have witnessed this scenario many times. It even happens to professionals. We have all seen players in the professional ranks achieve great success because of their physical ability, only to fall short in real-life situations. Ultimately, when the baseball career is over, it's how we act and interact with others that will count. Those who learn this lesson and live by it will become good coaches and teachers if they choose.

Play your role as a parent by teaching your child the proper response to praise and recognition: humility.

This is what often happens to young baseball players who lack humility: As years pass, other teammates with less ability but a better work ethic start to show more skill and pass them by. By working hard to get the most out of their ability, and through patience, their training in correct attitude and physical skills has paid off for them. Overconfident players who bask in their own glory eventually fall behind, especially if their teammates have the strength to remain humble and work hard to achieve sustainable skills. There are some players whose talent is great enough that they will succeed early on in spite of not being humble, but inevitably they alienate themselves from their teammates.

When kids first start out in baseball, some of them can naturally play better than others. Sometimes it's because they are physically gifted; other times it's just because they have matured earlier than the rest. At this early age, a parent's attitude about their kid's ability can play a huge role in how they develop as a ball player and, more importantly, as a person. If they appear to be one of the more talented players on the team, they will be in the spotlight early. Teach them to be responsible and to be a team player, not expecting special treatment, but fair treatment like everyone else. No matter what their level of ability, this is a great opportunity to show our kids how to take their God-given talents and use them for the good of others, by being a team player with humility. If you proceed without humility, your kid may have success for a while because they are talented, but here is the trap: Why be humble? Your child is already the best and in your mind will continue to be. (Don't confuse confidence with arrogance.) The problem with this approach is that, unless it's based on the sound training principle of *mind, body and technique to develop skill over time, it most likely will fail.* When early success is based on the fact that your child just happens to be bigger than other kids or has developed physically or mentally sooner than others, it can be deceiving if you are not familiar with real training concepts.

Lack of humility equals lack of learning.

I was watching a game one evening at the local youth baseball park and talking to a couple of fathers who had kids on the team. We were discussing hitting instruction while I was watching a kid at the plate who looked like he could use some. He had poor balance and his head was turning as he was basically swinging out of his shoes, although he did get lucky and hit the ball. One of the dads was bragging about how great his son was hitting and didn't see the need for any instruction. I was curious to see this kid so I asked him which boy was his. It was the six-year-old kid at the plate, and his name was Max.

Because Max hit the ball, his father equated that with success and assumed that it would continue because he was so gifted. As a hitting instructor, I noticed that Max hit the ball and I was happy for him, but I saw very little success in the mechanics of his swing, which is what one might expect from a six-year-old player. The problem is this: without some humility on the father's part, proper instruction may never happen. As Max grows older, he will eventually be playing against other players who developed their skill through proper training and the party will be over. Max won't be having much fun when he realizes that he cannot compete with the more skilled players. The father in this case was thinking "Why mess around with my son's swing when he is having such great success?" This kind of thinking is fueled by the need to feel instant gratification based on an outcome. It has nothing to do with being on a journey toward excellence.

Play your role as a parent by experiencing instant gratification one small achievement at a time as your child develops proper skills through efforts that will sustain them later in life.

Unfortunately, Max will probably have success for a few more years with this unbalanced, out-of-control swing, all the while ingraining incorrect techniques into his muscle memory. Other players, who have taken a more correct approach to training, will come to realize that real success happens over a period of time by accepting proper instruction instead of thinking they know it all. By adopting this humble attitude, they will develop real skills that will allow them to play at a higher level.

When your child is six-years-old, the coach is pitching the ball, and, in fact, is basically aiming at their bat, trying to help them hit the ball. If your child has any natural ability at all, they will hit some balls even with poor hitting mechanics. When they get older, it's a much different story. Pitchers who have developed their skill through proper training will be very successful striking out those hitters who have not trained properly.

Success at six-years-old and success at sixteen-years-old are two very different dynamics.

One will require excellent mechanics and the other will not. Good hitting, throwing, catching, base-running, and pitching mechanics do not "just happen." They must be developed through proper instruction over time and by repeating the correct physical motions over and over. Having the goal of becoming a better baseball player can, at times, be frustrating. It takes patience and *humility*.

When your child is struggling because they are new to baseball or they are smaller than other kids, it's easier to be humble. You see the need for instruction. You can't bear to watch your child fail over and over, so you proceed with humility and help them develop good habits in practice and attitude that will allow them to get the most out of their ability. These early struggles can be a blessing in disguise because you will be more inclined to seek out proper instruction at an early age, when the learning capabilities are at their peak.

The father mentioned earlier thought his six-year-old son, Max, already had it figured out just because he was hitting the ball (that was being carefully pitched by his very caring coach), so they are likely to miss a great learning opportunity. In a few years, the pitchers will not care if Max strikes out every time. By being humble, you will be less concerned with instant results like Max's father was, and more concerned with efforts that will bring your child eventual success. By practicing techniques that will develop skill, you and your child will be on the correct path of his baseball journey. The real gift of this correct approach is the growth of your child's confidence, and that often translates to good results on the field in a shorter period of time.

There are also those parents who refuse to see that their kids lack the natural ability or desire of others and, because of their own selfish desires or lack of understanding, will put unusual amounts of pressure on their child to succeed. All that this does is slow down their child's progress even more and may eventually sour them on the game. Many times, however, I see kids with less ability develop to their full potential over time and become very successful, while others with more natural talent—who had success early on—eventually are unsuccessful. I believe this has a lot to do with how their parent's attitude—humble or arrogant—influences them one way or another.

The need for humility is equally important whether your child has natural ability or not. Without it, it's just a matter of time until the talented kid gets a dose of reality. He will take success for granted. He is familiar with it. So far in his life, however, he is not familiar with failure. His arrogant and overprotective dad has made sure of that. What this dad has missed, however, is that if the skills needed to advance have not been fine-tuned along the way, and his son has just been relying on his natural ability to succeed over others with less ability, the journey will be cut short. The day will come when all the players on the team have similar abilities, and skill development or lack of it will be obvious.

It takes a lot of humility to admit that you need help when you have already experienced success. If you can do it, it's a sign of strength. It shows an awareness that you understand the process and are willing to take all the steps along the way to reach your full potential. I have had the opportunity to work with many young athletes over the years, but when it comes to humility, there is one who sticks in my mind.

Pierce, a very talented seventeen-year-old high school base-ball player, came to my gym seeking help. I had worked with several players his age, but what made Pierce different was that he had humility. He explained that he had not been hitting the ball well for a while and was not sure what to do about it. He said that he didn't think that he was seeing the ball well, and if you can't see it, you can't hit it. I had him hit a few balls off of the batting tee and his swing looked terrific. He knew the mechanics and performed them well. What Pierce could not do was make it happen during the game, when he felt pressure. It appeared to be more of a mental issue than one of incorrect hitting mechanics. I asked him what he was thinking while in the batter's box waiting for the pitch. He said, "I am thinking I have to get a hit." Since Pierce had proven himself in the past to be such a good hitter, he had been designated to be the clean-up man—the number four hitter in the line-up. He knew that it was his job to get hits to bring home the runners who were already on base. By putting pressure on himself, Pierce started thinking about the consequences of not getting a hit. Doing so placed his thinking in the future, not the present. Because of this thinking, his reflexes were too slow for the high level of competition and the pitcher won the battle.

We worked for an hour and he was one hundred percent at-tentive as I explained these philosophies to him. I also remind-ed him that the coach had him hitting in the clean-up position for a reason—he knew that he could hit, and that he had noth-ing to prove. By letting go of the pressure and not worrying about past failures or the hopes for the future, Pierce was able to stay "in the moment" and was able to turn things around. His concentration was better, and because of it, he could see the ball better as it left the pitcher's hand. The next day, Pierce hit the ball well. He was 3 for 4 as he helped his team get their first win of the season after going 0-7. He had changed his per-ception of the situation and turned pressure into challenge.

Not many kids of this age are looking for help with any-thing. I am sure that I was no different when I was seventeen.

But the sooner we learn to have humility, the sooner we can learn what we think we already know. I congratulated Pierce and let him know that his greatest success was being willing to show up for help.

A Lesson for Parents to Teach Young Ballplayers
You must have the confidence to focus on your own effort and stay the course with your training and not be concerned if someone else has some temporary advantage over you. Who knows; maybe they have no humility and are going nowhere. You don't know. You shouldn't care. Their effort is their own and so is yours. Have a vision. Do you want to excel at a high level? Then you must train and be willing to continue to develop skills that you appear to already be good at.

If you are not humble and are puffing your chest out at your current level, you will progress slowly—or not at all—and time will decide your fate. Instead, use the passage of time to your advantage by being open-minded, learning all that you can, and having fun along the way. It's not a competition with others. It's only a competition with yourself. You are the one you must conquer: your attitude, your fears, your doubts. Remember, many things can change over time. Other people whom you thought were your rivals may quit for various reasons. Some will eventually drop out because their skills are not developed and they can no longer compete with those who have trained properly.

Others will lose the love of the game because their parents or coaches overdid it and burned them out, or they may simply realize that their passion lies elsewhere. Do not be overly concerned with what others are doing or getting, that you are not. If you are, you are likely to make excuses and blame others for your own lack of effort. You will begin to see only what you are not getting, instead of appreciating what you have already gotten.

It's not flattering to see a child carry this attitude into adulthood. It's like being on a treadmill. You are going nowhere fast! When you are making excuses and blaming others, you aren't learning a thing. The humble approach would be to acknowledge another person's achievement and realize that you too can choose to put forth the required effort to attain your own goals. If you still have the love for the game, if you still have your health and the fitness necessary to excel at your passion, be thankful and learn all you can.

Focus on your own effort, be humble, and quit saying "I know."

Chapter 7

Be the Example

A Parent's Role in Leading by Example: be a good example not only to kids, but to other parents.

It's nothing new to say that adults should set a good example for young people. I think that most people do a pretty good job at it in general. But many parents find it hard to do when the competition starts. It's a real test of character to sit and watch as the umpire makes a bad call, especially when it affects your child in a strikeout or a close play at a base. But should we react by yelling out negative phrases for all to hear? I have seen this too many times. It's pretty common. What kind of example have we set in this situation?

It's not easy, but we should try hard to stay positive, because every time our kids hear us grow negative and make excuses, it reinforces this very behavior in them. Many times the same people who have set a good example for their kids on the way to the ballpark by driving safely and obeying all the rules of the road lose their perspective once they get to the field and the competition starts. They may have even shown consideration to other drivers on the way to the park by letting them go first or engaging in some other act of kindness. But once the game starts, they are disrespecting the umpire when they don't get their way. It's also interesting to note that many parents and coaches who display this negative attitude will reprimand young players if they do the same.

If one minute you are insisting on respect and the next minute you are being disrespectful yourself, your kids receive mixed signals. If you are a coach, you will lose credibility with your players; if you are a parent, you will lose credibility with your child.

Do we act responsibly when we get our way or when things are going well, but suddenly display immature behavior when our expectations are not met? There's already a natural tendency for a child to do that and now, by our poor example, we are giving that tendency some credibility. A very familiar scenario for coaches is to witness the entire group of parents acting responsibly at the parent meeting—saying things like, "it's for the kids"—before the season starts, and then watch some parents turn into ranting and raving maniacs once the competition starts. Kids are pretty perceptive. It can be very embarrassing for players to sit in the dugout and hear their parents being negative and disrespectful in the stands.

Play your role as a parent by displaying strong character, whether things are going well or poorly. Strong character will help your child become a better ballplayer. It will also help them become a better person.

There are many pitfalls and traps that parents should learn to avoid as young athletes pursue their interests or maybe even *passions* in sports. Blaming the umpires is one of the biggest offenses. It never helps you win the game. *It only shows your kids how to disrespect authority and blame others for their own weaknesses.* You may not think so, but your kids will pick up on this negative behavior and it will affect their own attitude about umpires. Many times, after a loss, I have overheard kids say, "The umps lost that one for us!" As long as a kid believes this, they will not grow as a player. And if fate does not allow for an enlightened coach or some other adult to affect them in a more positive way, making excuses will become a normal response when things don't go their way.

This is a losing way.

When parents and coaches show a good example by staying positive and focus on things over which they have some control, such as their own good effort, players will learn to follow that example and accept the fact that some close calls by the umpire will not go their way. They'll learn that you have to be able to absorb a few bad calls by the ump and still be able to win if you are striving to be the best. *This is a winning way.*

How about when parents from the other team become really vocal and are questioning every call by the ump? They may even be directing their anger towards your team or your own child. This can be very distracting. Are you going to get in a verbal debate with them that can actually get physical? This can happen really quickly. I have seen it. You may have heard about these situations or seen them on the evening news. They can get ugly. How to be an example in this case would be to say nothing. There is nothing to say. You are not dealing with rational people when you are talking about adults losing their tempers at a kids' game in which the only goal should be having fun, adults and kids having fun together, both teams having fun together, cooperating for the sake of the young athletes on the field.

Do you want to show your child that you are willing to confront irrational people, just because your ego won't let you do otherwise? Wouldn't your advice to them be to just walk away if someone wants to fight at school? Yet, are you willing to be the example and just let it go and not take it personally at a ball game when someone says something bad about your kid?

This is a great opportunity to play your role as a parent by showing your young athlete by example that other people's bad behavior has nothing to do with us—or our good efforts.

Don't get sucked in. Be a good example when negative things happen and help your young players stay focused on their own effort and correct attitude. If you can do this, *even if you lose a game in which the other team behaved poorly, you will have achieved a higher victory.* Helping your kids build good character over time is much more important than any single win!

A baseball game is a great place for kids to see all kinds of examples being set, good and bad. Which one will you be? We have a choice as to how we are going to act. Many times I hear athletes or coaches say these words emphatically: "I hate to lose!" They say them and make sure that other people hear them. They may think it shows people how much they care. But what are they really saying? Maybe they are saying "I can't take losing and I have to win in order to feel good about myself." No one actually *likes* to lose, but it's a fact of life that it will happen sometimes. Every team that has won the World Series lost several games during the regular season, but it didn't stop them from becoming World Champions.

As a parent sitting in the stands, if you haven't done a little soul-searching in this area, you might find yourself setting a bad example if winning is the only thing that matters. If your focus and your measure of success are only on the winning of the game or a winning season, then you are likely to miss any other learning or life lessons that can benefit your child.

Success in life is always preceded by ups and downs, just like in a baseball game. Why not let your child experience both the ups and downs for what they really are—reality?

Play your role as a parent by teaching your child that the way to feel good about yourself is to put forth a consistent good effort and that complaining and making excuses is not productive.

In a post-game interview on the radio after losing the championship game, I heard a college coach comment that the season was a failure because they didn't win the big one. I thought, "What a shame that he didn't celebrate all the successes that got the team to the championship game in the first place!" Perhaps winning the championship would have looked good on the coach's resume, but for most of the players, their careers as athletes would soon be over and that game would not have much impact on their lives; the good effort that it took to get to that game would.

There can be many reasons why you do not win any one game. One reason might be that, on that day, the other team was just better. We should respect that. On a college level and even more so in the pros, it's understandable that the ultimate goal is winning it all. It's what coaches and players are recruited or paid to do. Still, it's refreshing to hear certain coaches lead by example at this high level by saying something like "We did all we could do; so did the other team, and today, they won."

There's nothing wrong with wanting or trying to win a championship, but trying our best to do it is all that we can do. If this was accomplished and you still lost the championship game, I do not see the season as a failure. A lot of successes happened along the way to get to that championship game. It's those individual successes that should be celebrated when kids are young, not some coach or parent acting like it's the end of the world because we lost a game! Unfortunately, when this "win it all" mentality is present in youth sports, it takes the focus away from the most important element of competition—*effort!* The result of this instant-gratification attitude by coaches and parents is always negative. Confidence is shattered when adults expect too much too soon from kids. It's almost impossible for a young player to understand the concept of taking one step at a time on their journey toward excellence when the adults in their lives are only concerned with winning right now. When this happens, personal achievement (effort) is being minimalized, while winning (outcome) is being emphasized. This approach doesn't lead anywhere good when kids are young and trying to develop skill and confidence. It only leads to disappointment, and for many, giving up.

The importance of building confidence cannot be overstated. The way to build confidence is through personal effort at practice and by working on skill development, not by being on the so-called "best travel team." Too much emphasis on winning is distracting for a young, inexperienced player who is still developing the skills needed to win. Many times I have heard parents say to their kids "It's not about winning; it's about having fun." This is a correct statement made by many parents who, once the competition starts, become the worst possible example by screaming at umpires, disrespecting the coach, and coming up with every excuse in the book when their team is losing. Winning a game or a championship at any level is exciting, but many parents and youth coaches do not understand that developing personal skills is *real* success and it's what will help every player contribute to the team and ultimately prepare for the future.

If kids see too much disappointment from the adults around them after losing a game, they will start to equate success only with winning the game. Why wouldn't they? This is the disappointing example we are showing them, and it can cause young players to become result-oriented instead of focusing on effort. They will start looking for shortcuts; they will get lost. If kids playing the game are always concerned about the outcome because they know their parents or coaches put winning first, they will play tight, try too hard, and lose focus. This will result in even less wins than if, by example, the adults around them would just show kids how to deal with losing by staying positive and having the discipline to remain focused on effort.

By being a good example, praising the other team for playing well, and explaining to your players how they can go about strengthening certain points of their game or personal technique, you can instill in them a good work ethic. They won't believe it, though, unless you do the same in your own life. Kids are smart and very perceptive. They will think that you are just trying to make them feel good after they experience failure and they will be right unless you "practice what you preach." Failure is natural. It happens to everyone. It's what you do or how you act afterwards that counts.

Be the example!

Play your role as a parent or coach and show your kids by example how to deal with failure in a positive way. Teach them that real failure is wanting success without wanting to do the work.

While serving as the hitting coach for a local high school, I witnessed how setting a poor example can have a very negative affect on a very good team. The head coach in this case was the team's biggest liability. His whole approach to coaching was negative and arguing with umpires was common, even though he was also an experienced umpire. At first, the players thought that it was cute when the coach would prance around like a banty rooster, ranting and raving over what he thought were bad calls by the ump. At times, he was even ejected from the game. Soon, the players started to mimic the coach's behavior, but were reprimanded by him for doing so. Basically, he demanded respect from players but was very disrespectful himself.

Finally, the players saw through his circus act and tried their best to stay positive with the help of the assistant coaches. The unfortunate result of the coach's negative behavior, however, was the eventual failure of a very talented team, which included eight seniors. At the beginning of the season the team had been considered a favorite to go to the state tournament. Not only did this not happen, but they had a losing season. They didn't even play well enough to get into the very first tournament to determine the district champions, and the season ended in great disappointment.

The coach's negative attitude not only affected the players, but it affected his own performance as a coach. This man was a very talented ballplayer himself, but always responded in a negative manner when a close call by the umpire didn't go his way or even if the other team scored. He had a tendency to give up. It was common to see him with his head in his hands in the first inning if the other team scored first. The players noticed this and would comment, "Well, coach has already thrown in the towel!"

It's easy to just blame the coach in instances like this, but many times the schools that hire them fail to see that the skills to teach young players by example are not there. Having baseball skills and knowledge is nice, but it did nothing for the eight talented seniors who watched their final year of high school baseball squandered by a coach whose ego would not allow him the humility to lead by example.

Leading by example should be the goal of every parent, whether they know something about baseball or not. There's nothing more pathetic to watch than a parent (who knows nothing about what it takes to become proficient at a difficult sport like baseball) boldly express their opinion on how things should be done to an experienced coach or teacher. These opinions are usually born out of a need by certain parents for instant gratification or an out-of-control ego. Parents such as these are not playing their role very well and their child's progress in baseball will suffer because of it.

"Inspiring" is the word that comes to mind when you come across parents who are willing to learn their role as a parent, because they understand this simple concept: *that anything that is difficult takes time.* These parents are on a path to happiness and their kids will follow. They are showing their child by example that when you're on a journey you should enjoy the ride and not count on outcomes to make you happy. They understand that we have no control over outcomes (future), only effort (now). They also know that it's important to be aware of what we know and what we don't know, and have the humility to stay on the path by accepting criticism and help from others more experienced than ourselves. This is what is known as *the parent's role in their child's journey.*

Chapter 8

Self-Discipline

A Parent's Role in Helping Their Kids Develop Self-Discipline: be consistent with your own self-discipline.

Self-discipline is the ability to be consistent; without it, it's difficult, if not impossible, to reach one's full potential.

We become disciplined through our experience. Were we taught by our own parents to have discipline or were we taught to make excuses and look for the easy way? If we were taught, as we were growing up, that we should be consistent in putting forth good effort with our activities, and our parents showed us through their own actions that being disciplined and consistent can pay off, we are very fortunate. We can now pass that on to our own kids.

Not everyone gets this experience at an early age, however, so becoming a disciplined person can be tough. It's not easy to excel at something which is difficult. You must be consistent. To be consistent, you must have discipline. To develop discipline and *really* have it, you must be consistent. As you can see, they go hand-in-hand. So how can we teach our kids to get the most out of their ability? Self-motivation is the key. They are on a journey—a journey to achieve excellence at something. It may be to achieve the rank of black belt in karate. It may be to play baseball at a high level. Later in life it will be getting a job they like and having a successful family life. Without self-discipline, *they will not make it;* they will always look for shortcuts and make excuses. They will be on a journey of mediocrity, or worse, failure.

I am often reminded of a friend of mine, Jim Huot-Vickery, who, along with Anna Shallman, traveled 1,100 miles by canoe from International Falls, Minnesota, to the Hudson Bay. I don't know the details of the trip, but I can only imagine that there were a lot of unknown circumstances and dangers along the way as they paddled through miles of wilderness alone, without the benefit of modern conveniences to help them along. Experience had taught them that having the discipline to stay consistent with a routine is what they could rely on. Taking a trip of this magnitude is not for everyone, only the experienced. Lack of discipline on their part could have cost my friend and his companion their lives had they taken off unprepared. Everything we do in our lives is like this canoe trip through the wilderness. There are a lot of unknowns in the world. If we are to expect success, no matter how large or small the task, we must have the discipline to prepare and stay prepared.

Discipline doesn't just "show up." You learn it while on your journey to excellence. By self-motivating, little by little, you condition yourself away from the old way of thinking to a new more enlightened way of being. Your passion for the activity will play a big role. If a kid has little passion for something but has been coaxed or forced to do it, it will be hard, if not impossible, for them to develop self-discipline. They are more likely to develop resentment. This is a good thing to remember when we sign our kids up for baseball, or any activity for that matter. In the beginning it's hard to tell if there really is a passion that exists because kids tend to like anything that is new. Remember, a kid's passion is having fun!

I loved baseball growing up, so I thought that it would be a good idea to expose my son Phillip to it at an early age. At four-years-old, I was pretty convinced that he would like it, but I was basing that assumption on absolutely nothing. Or was I? There is a natural tendency to live through our children.

I was not yet aware of his natural tendencies towards athletics or anything for that matter. I admit that I was quite pleased when I realized that he loved baseball! Because he loved it, he wanted to practice (play) every day, even at four-years-old. As years passed and he got older, it took more discipline on his part, because other things were competing for his attention. As it turns out, the passion for baseball had grown in him and he managed to make time to practice, along with his many other activities. Not to say that I didn't have to nudge him along a little bit. Kids won't love everything that we get them into, but when they do love something, we must play our role and encourage them and sacrifice our time for them whenever possible.

I have a karate student named Dale. At twelve-years-old, he is displaying the kind of attitude toward training that will take him far not only in martial arts, but in life. He comes to class on a consistent basis and pays attention while he is there. When I first met Dale, he was a baseball student of mine. He was actually pretty good at that as well, but his interest level dropped for some reason. There was no negative situation that caused him to stop as far as I could tell. He just decided that it wasn't for him. He still enjoyed baseball, but in a different way. He became an umpire and is quite good at it. Dale has realized that his real passion lies in karate training. Like baseball, karate requires a lot of time and effort spent on training to become proficient. They are identical in the sense that one must repeat the correct motions over and over until they are automatic and can be executed without thinking. Without proper training, thinking will always be present and reaction time will be too slow to compete at a high level. Dale understands this dynamic and will take advantage of every opportunity that comes his way. If I say that I am offering extra training for those who are getting ready to test for a higher level, Dale is there, or as he puts it: "I'm in!" There is one other huge reason why Dale will get to where he is going on his martial arts journey: his parents play their role very well.

One night, when Dale's class had finished and he was walking out the door, he realized that no one else was coming in the door for the scheduled adult class. Instead of continuing to his dad's car he turned and asked me, "Sensei ["teacher" in Japanese], what do you do if no one shows up for class?" I told him that I usually use the time for personal training. Then I realized what he was getting at, so I asked him if he wanted to stick around for a private session. He said "Yes, definitely; let me ask my dad." His dad said "No problem, I will come back in an hour." The significant thing to realize here is the role the parent played. Many parents would say, "No we've got to get going, I have things to do!" In this case, Dale's father recognized his son's passion and was willing to inconvenience himself by changing his schedule, driving home and coming back so that Dale could receive extra training. It's a sacrifice that many parents are unwilling to make for selfish reasons, or they remain unaware of the discipline that it takes to achieve excellence. This is a great example of how a parent can play a role in their child's development in karate, baseball, or any other activity in which their child shows an interest. By having the self-discipline to look past his own needs, Dale's father has played his role in helping his son take the necessary steps toward his goal: becoming a black belt in karate.

Self-motivation is a great tool when it comes to developing self-discipline. Sometimes you just don't feel like working out. It would be easy to not do it. Someone motivates you, or you motivate yourself and you do it anyway. By doing this, you come to realize that you are never sorry. You never say to yourself, "What a mistake; I shouldn't have worked out." Motivating yourself toward your goal by getting in that workout when you would rather be doing something else that requires less effort is always rewarding. It's a reminder of where you are heading on your journey: how far you have come, and how far you have yet to go. Once again, you become aware that effort leads to change and you become more disciplined each time you motivate yourself to put forth the effort. Obviously, if you are injured or really sick, it may be better to wait.

Usually, this is not the case when we talk ourselves out of training; we're just being lazy. By helping kids remember their outward goal (the end of their journey), it motivates them to want to get there. But instead of only dreaming about the future goal, show them how to get there; show them that the path to excellence is by way of their inward goal: taking the next step. When the steps are difficult and frustrating, teach them the life lesson of self-motivation, which will lead to self-discipline. By doing this, a person can stay on the path, and as their passion grows, so does their chance for success: in baseball, and life.

If your approach to your child's baseball experience is to try to influence coaches so they will give your kid opportunities, you are not playing your role very well. You may get a result that serves *you* now, but not your child in the future. Playing politics is not sustainable; personal effort is. Teach your child that a consistent good effort on their part is what will eventually bring them opportunities and you will be playing your role as a parent very well. Not only does this require discipline, but it requires patience because many times we do not get opportunities when we want them. When parents have an "instant gratification" attitude, the whole process is sabotaged. With this attitude, you will be teaching your child that they must have success right away to please you. You are basically saying to your child that, as a parent, you have not developed the discipline to have patience and let the process work over time. If you are blaming others for your child's lack of success, you will be telling your child that making excuses is okay. If this is the case, how can you expect your child to have self-discipline when it comes to trying to excel at baseball? Be careful; they will naturally follow your lead.

Play your role as a parent by having discipline as it applies to your child's baseball journey. Resist playing politics with coaches, giving your child the freedom to develop sustainable skills through self-discipline.

There is nothing more concerning than to hear a young player speaking badly of a coach or an umpire in language that you would normally hear an adult use. I have witnessed this several times over the years, but rarely from a kid who has been taught by his parents to have respect. Kids whose parents have the discipline to teach them to have respect for others instead of blaming others are very lucky. In turn, they will learn this life lesson themselves and become players with strength of mind, developing a good work ethic instead of looking for the easy way. By developing self-discipline, your child will become a leader and others will be influenced in a positive way by their behavior. The more disciplined you become, the more aware you become of others with discipline or lack of discipline. This is a valuable tool if you are a coach or teacher. If you have very little restraint yourself, you will be ineffective as a teacher or coach because there is no perspective to start from. Coaches who lack discipline themselves are likely to be inconsistent when it comes to disciplining their players. In order to win, they will overlook poor attitude from a gifted player but reprimand the whole team when things are going bad. They don't recognize the situation for what it really is: lack of respect! When respect is absent, there won't be much harmony among the players, coaches, and parents.

Without self-discipline, talented players are on the road to mediocrity. The talent that works for them today will be useless in the future, when they are competing against others who take a more disciplined, respectful approach. You often see this in youth baseball when the focus is on winning. Coaches, who are willing to overlook poor behavior from the star player, lack the fortitude to do the right thing: sit them on the bench!

Players, who are receiving preferential treatment when they are young just because they are talented, are on a failed mission. If they are not required to develop self-discipline, the day will come when they will have to stand on their own and they will be lost. With little or no training in the life lesson of humility, it will be a wake-up call when their talent is no longer enough. Every year we see this in professional sports. Athletes, who have reached the very top and are big stars, eventually self-destruct because of a lack of discipline, and they become arrogant and self-absorbed. Those who have developed discipline and humility in their personal and professional lives go on to have long and productive careers, and give of their time to help others.

Playing baseball can take up a lot of time in a person's life. It's a wonderful sport and a lot of fun to play. Many people start at age five and play for fifteen to twenty years. If you end up playing for that long, chances are that you will learn something about having discipline, unless you are one of those gifted players who receives special treatment in spite of a poor attitude. For most people, baseball is too difficult a sport to be able to continue playing without self-discipline. Those who are not held accountable for poor behavior and lack of effort when they are young will likely drop out when the going gets tough. Because they were never taught to have respect and work hard, it will be easy for them to make excuses, blame others, and move on to less challenging activities.

One day, everyone faces the fact that they have grown up and are left with whatever life lessons were taught to them when they were young. Hopefully, having self-discipline was one of those lessons because just having natural talent will not take them very far in baseball, or in life.

Chapter 9

Self-Confidence

A Parent's Role in Helping Their Kids Gain Confidence: keep a proper perspective about competition so that kids can gain confidence, one achievement at a time.

Self-confidence is one of those things that some people have a lot of, and others seem to have very little of, but that all of us are capable of. It's having confidence in one's own judgment, ability, power, decisions, etc.

Our own experience growing up can affect how our confidence level will either grow or not grow. Or maybe even diminish. I remember growing up on our family farm. My brothers and I were taught many skills at an early age that had to do with operating all kinds of machinery and tools. We were also taught how to care for animals that we had on the farm. With so many different tasks to be completed on a daily basis, we became very competent helpers for our parents who were skilled teachers of confidence, not giving us tasks that would overwhelm us and shatter our self-assurance before we were prepared to handle them. We were basically taught to be confident out of necessity: confident in ourselves, each other, and our tools. Farming is a dangerous business, so we would graduate through the different phases, starting with caring for small animals and equipment when we were very young, to handling cattle and large farm machinery by the time we were teenagers.

The point is that young people are very capable of developing a high level of skill and responsibility if given the chance. But proper direction is the key. We cannot expect kids to 'just do it" as is the case so often at Little League fields across the country. High expectations without proper instruction can shatter a kid's self-confidence. Demanding too much too soon can put excessive pressure on kids that they may not be prepared to handle.

Balance is the key. Play your role as a parent by putting forth the effort to find it.

Self-confidence will either grow or diminish based on two dynamics. First, if nothing is ever expected of kids, they have very little chance of gaining confidence. If parents let them off the hook when they misbehave, or make excuses for them when they fail, they will gain the *false confidence* that someone will always cover for them. The day will come when their parents are not there to make things right for them, and they may be ill-prepared to show confidence later in life when most needed. When we treat kids like this, *it's like we don't expect them to grow up and become adults.* Without realizing it, they will fail to develop the confidence needed to act correctly when faced with adversity, or bad situations.

Second, if parents expect too much too soon from kids, and expect them to perform like miniature adults, it's hard for them to gain their own confidence as well, because they will be set up for failure, since they are not prepared for the task and will be trying to live up to their parents' unrealistic expectations.

Confidence Is Gained a Little at a Time

One day, at my hitting school, during a class with nine-year-old boys, we were working on the technique of hitting the ball using a pitching machine. One boy, Jake, was struggling with this new skill that we were learning. His dad finally decided to point out to me all the different things that he was doing wrong with his mechanics. I replied with, "He's doing alright. New things can take some time." The boy's father said, "No, he just won't do what he is told." I was a bit shocked by his lack of patience and need for instant results and felt like saying, "Why don't you jump in there and let me speed the machine up to about 80 mph and I'll tell you to 'just hit it' and see how you do." I didn't say anything to him, but instead decided to direct some positive reinforcement towards Jake so that he could develop some confidence in the new task of hitting the ball from the pitching machine. Positive reinforcement builds self-confidence; lack of patience with a young player shatters self-confidence.

The biggest mistake I see parents and coaches make in the development of a young player's confidence is expecting them to be good at something that they have not practiced enough. Baseball is a tough game to play at every level; kids can't "just be confident" because we tell them to. When coaches and parents lose patience during games because the players can't make the plays or hit the ball, their usual response is to start yelling, as if the players are failing intentionally. Who likes being yelled at? It's not like they misbehaved and needed an attitude correction. *The kids want to play baseball because it is fun, not so they can have a bunch of adults yell at them.* They get yelled at because the adults want success now. When young, inexperienced players are yelled at, they usually start playing worse because whatever confidence they did have is now compromised because of fear of failure. They are trying to live up to someone else's expectations.

With kids, it's important to be able to tell the difference between an experienced player who lacks focus and a beginner who lacks skill, so that the correct instruction or advice can be given. I have coached plenty of players who had talent and ability, but lacked confidence. Some of these talented young players had the added burden of high expectations on their shoulders, put there by adults. If kids haven't practiced and developed the correct technique, they will have very little confidence that they can do it in a game when there is pressure. Their intuition is correct, but they may not know the reason they lack confidence. Unfortunately, this sometimes results in the young players being too hard on themselves. All kids need correct instruction at practice, not adults putting their own unrealistic expectations on display by yelling like maniacs when an error is made. Once again, this just sounds like good common sense, but go out to a ball field where there is competition, and emotions out of control, and good old-fashioned common sense can be hard to find.

Play your role as a parent by letting knowledge be your guide, not emotions.

One season, when I was coaching a team of nine and ten-year-olds, I had a player named Nick who was afraid of being hit by the ball. On the one hand, how could you blame him? Nick was just nine-years-old and still trying to develop confidence as a hitter. The pitcher he was facing was also nine-years-old, and being the first year of kid pitch baseball, had little or no experience, and probably little or no correct instruction in pitching. In other words, like most nine-year-old kids in this situation, he couldn't really do it. Nick is a pretty smart kid and he instinctively knew the chance of getting hit by the ball thrown by this very inexperienced pitcher was good. This was no longer the coach or his dad pitching.

Nick was also a student of mine at Chuck's Gym, and I was working with him to help him overcome his fear. One day his mother met me as I was walking toward the field to get ready for the game. She had a very good perspective about her son's baseball experience and expressed her concern about Nick still being afraid after a few games. Her question was "What can we do about Nick being afraid of the ball?" My answer was "Nothing. We have done and are doing everything we can for Nick by staying positive, being encouraging, and teaching him techniques to avoid being hit in the face or other vulnerable areas. Once the game starts, it's up to Nick. He must be the one to find the courage to stay in there and try his best to hit the ball. We can't do that for him."

Nick did find his courage eventually. A year later, I was at a game watching a couple of my students, and a player walked up to the plate very confidently and, on a 3-2 count, hit a line drive past the second baseman. As this player was walking back to the dugout after scoring on the next play, he took his helmet off and once again I was reminded what can happen when parents are patient and stay positive. The player was Nick. By being patient and staying positive, Nick's parents helped him gain confidence. If these two things are understood and accepted by the parent and the player, progress will be made by practicing basic technique.

Nick's experience is a great example of a parent patiently playing their role in a positive and encouraging way that can help their child on their baseball journey.

When basic skills start developing through many correct repetitions, more advanced technique can be attempted. *Through this process, confidence will grow like a seed being planted in the ground.* There are no shortcuts. When looking for shortcuts, what you usually find is failure. Sure, something might happen that makes you feel good for the moment, but by taking shortcuts, do you really learn the route? One day, you will need to perform at a level you are not prepared for, and things might not go well. Others will have developed skills that you do not have. They didn't take the shortcuts and are on a path that you don't recognize because you haven't been on it. The path to excellence consists of many steps and when parents get in the way of their child's progress by making excuses for them, never letting them experience failure, buying them the most expensive bat thinking that this is what will make them a good hitter…. You get the point.

These are all attempted shortcuts that will get you lost every time. Remaining patient and encouraging young players to stay on the path of their baseball journey will help them experience joy, have fun, and gain confidence. They will gain confidence in their own skills by practicing correct technique, and be assured that their parents and coaches will allow them to grow at their own pace, instead of overreacting emotionally at games when things don't go well. Once confidence is developed, the success will take care of itself. It will show up not only on the baseball field, but other areas of their life as well. Without self-confidence, how can you expect to have success at your job, in school, learning new skills, or in your relationships?

Whether you realize it or not, as the parent or coach of a young baseball player, you are affecting kids by your own behavior. When coaches act like drill sergeants while working with young kids, it will stifle the kids' creativity and cause them to act out of fear instead of confidence. Macho parents and coaches who take the stereotypical "no pain, no gain" approach to teaching young kids, before the kids are ready for it, are just showing everyone it's about themselves and not the kids. If you want to be a drill sergeant, join the Army. Young, inexperienced players will not respond well to this "in your face" approach. Most likely, it will shatter their confidence and they may decide that baseball is not for them. Older, more experienced players may be motivated by such tactics, but the best approach is to show players how to be their own drill sergeant by teaching them to self-motivate. This is a lesson that is sustainable for a lifetime; you no longer need someone to "drill it" into you. The only way this works is if coaches and parents learn the fine art of motivating kids instead of alienating them. As it turns out, it's an art that can be easy to learn if you have humility, patience, perspective, and the desire to help kids gain confidence one step at a time. If you do not have these character traits, motivating kids will be impossible and you are not a youth coach. If you do have them, I encourage you to educate yourself about baseball in every way you can. There are numerous books and DVDs available that teach the basics of hitting, pitching, fielding, base running and coaching techniques. There are also more knowledgeable coaches than yourself who will gladly share their experiences if you have the humility to listen. These days, there is no excuse for showing up at the ball field unprepared to teach basics to the age group you will be coaching. If you are unprepared as a coach, you are likely to confuse and alienate players more than you help them. You will be ineffective as a coach and your players' confidence will suffer because of it.

A student of mine, Steven, had been "struggling to hit the ball lately," according to his father. When they came to Steven's lesson, his father was a bit beside himself about the fact that Steven had been doing so well, but suddenly couldn't seem to hit the ball at all. He couldn't figure it out. While he was verbally analyzing the situation looking for a solution and hoping for some enlightened answer from me, the hitting coach, I couldn't help thinking about the impact he may be having on his son. How this father reacts to the process of learning a skill will affect his son's confidence in a positive way or a negative way. He shared with me that Steven did fine while hitting off the batting tee and during the soft toss drills, but hitting the pitches during the game—where there is pressure—is where things went bad.

He wanted an answer.

I gave it to him. I said, "He's seven."

Chapter 10

Pressure or Challenge

A Parent's Role in Helping Kids Deal With Pressure: do not expect immediate results and let kids have fun, developing over time, through correct training.

Practicing in the batting cage and playing in the game are very different dynamics. You are swinging a bat in both situations, trying for that perfect swing, but one thing is different when it's time to compete—pressure.

Pressure from parents and coaches will cause a young player to think about results, which will adversely affect their performance. Stress and anxiety cause them to tighten up, and will slow reflexes, something a baseball player can't afford. When this happens, overthinking has become their reality instead of just reacting, and failure is usually the result. This can happen to a big-leaguer also, and the cause is probably the pressure of maintaining such a high level of performance against the best players in the world. When a kid feels pressured while playing a game, most likely the cause is adults who lose control of their emotions and have a tendency to turn a game into something it's not—a job.

The message we are sending young players when we pressure them is that we are concerned about the outcome, which, of course, is in the future. We must remember that we're not living in the future but right now, and how we perceive "right now" can have an effect on the future. If a player's perception of "right now" is a feeling of pressure, he or she will probably not react correctly to the ball being pitched at them or when throwing and catching on defense. In other words, the good outcome we were trying to force by applying pressure is less likely to happen than if we were to just let the kids play and have fun.

"When your body, feet, and hands act without your doing anything in your mind, you make no misses, ten times out of ten." This was written by Miyamoto Musashi—an undefeated, masterless samurai—in 1643. Sounds easy enough, right? If you've ever tried to hit a baseball, however, you know that it's not easy at all. Getting three hits out of ten tries is considered excellent. If your goal is to play at a very high level, such as in college or professionally, you need to be consistent at letting the mind do what the body knows. In other words, if you think you are trying to hit the baseball while in the batter's box, your results will be inconsistent; you will be adding pressure. If you forget consciousness of hitting and hit in a normal frame of mind, you will be steady. Through correct practice on mechanics and conditioning, skill develops to the point that correct technique has become normal.

If this effort in practice does not equal the difficulty of the task, however, it will be normal for you to fail.

Musashi puts it this way: "When the effects of exercise build up unawares and practice accumulates, thoughts of wishing to quickly develop skill disappear quietly, and whatever you do, you spontaneously become free from conscious thoughts."

Every competitive situation has a certain amount of pressure that is real. You can't change it; you can only prepare for it.

Lack of preparation invites pressure to dominate you. If kids can learn to perceive their present competitive situation as a challenge, they can gain focus and increase their successes. By being adequately prepared through proper training, a player will learn to turn a pressure situation into a challenge, giving themselves a chance for success. As a player grows older, if they have done their work, they will be prepared to deal with pressure. If they haven't done their work, they face a real possibility of failure.

Many young players, when they fail in an at-bat or on defense, feel even more pressure the next time a ball is coming their way. At their young age, they lack perspective, so they let the pressure build up instead of letting it go. Even worse, if they hear their parent's voice from the stands or their coach responding in a negative way, they will be left in the dark, with no instruction and with no hope of doing better next time. When kids make an error, if all they hear is, "C'mon, you gotta have that one"; you are not challenging them, you are pressuring them. You can challenge them by giving them instructions about the error and a solution for how to improve for the future. Just yelling at kids will not work; it just shows others how little *you* know.

When working with young players, it's important for coaches to create pressure situations in practice and then teach the kids how to deal with it. In order for this to be effective, however, coaches need to be knowledgeable about the techniques themselves; otherwise, the kids will be left with the pressure and no solution. When we create pressure situations in practice, we are creating teaching moments. This is a great time for kids to experience a little failure under our guidance. Some parents, who have respect for this approach, will realize the need for correct training and decide to take action by practicing more with their kids. Others will cling to their need for instant gratification; they will make excuses when their child experiences failure, blame coaches, and just continue *hoping* for success.

During practice is also a great time to teach perspective. The best way to teach it is to have good perspective ourselves by remembering that kids will not play perfectly. An example of good perspective would be to see the big picture and not dwell on every little failure. When we dwell on failures and fail to give proper instruction to kids, we are adding pressure.

"Throw strikes!" is not proper instruction when a young pitcher is failing to get the ball over the plate.

"Stay loose; remember to breathe" would be better advice; the kid knows he's supposed to throw strikes.

"Get mad at the ball!" is another one you hear from parents and coaches who do not understand that a football mentality does not work when a kid is failing to hit the baseball. They seem to be suggesting that by swinging harder, the child will have a better chance of making contact with the ball. But quite the opposite is true as the mechanics of the swing break down because of an over-aggressive, out-of-control motion.

"See the ball; hit the ball," as Pete Rose used to say, is a better, simpler approach. You have to see it before you can hit it and when young kids over-swing they also pull their eyes off the path of the ball by turning their head. I often ask a young player who their favorite major-league player is. If they say Derek Jeter, I ask them, "How do you think Derek Jeter would hit if he was blindfolded?" They usually respond with, "He would miss the ball." "Why?" I ask. Every time the young player will say, "Because he can't see it." In Derek Jeter's case, the ball being pitched by a major-leaguer gets to him in less than one half-second and, if he turns his head instead of bringing it down while he swings, he is essentially blindfolded.

Remember, skills are developed at practice, not in games. In a game, a player will swing a bat just a few times. At practice, that same player can build muscle memory by swinging correctly 100 times. By doing this on a consistent basis, there will be less pressure during the game because the swing has become automatic. They don't have to think about it; it has become part of them. Challenge kids to see the ball come out of your hand or out of the pitching machine by first focusing their eyes on the logo on your cap and then picking up the ball at the release point. By picking up the ball immediately instead of halfway to home plate, the player has more time to determine location. As they grow older and face experienced pitchers, they will also need to determine speed. Now, when they are struggling in a game, you can offer some real information that will have meaning to them: "See the ball." This works better than some vague command like "get mad at the ball!" Without this training, all your child will have is whatever they had during the last game, maybe even less because it is what you do *after* you fail that counts. If you do nothing but expect different results next time, all you will get is more pressure next time. As time passes, confidence is gained by taking those correct swings at practice and a player will ultimately feel challenged instead of pressured when the game begins. When we focus on the big picture (the journey) we are creating challenge. If we teach kids to see the big picture, they will learn to let go of the disappointments more quickly; they will realize that some failure is normal. Eventually, they will learn to trust that by being consistent with good effort, failure is only a part of the process, not who they are.

Kids are very aware of how the adults around them react when they fail, although they don't always show it. If adults react negatively when a young player experiences failure, that young player will react by trying to live up to the adult's expectations, which are often unrealistic. If this negative behavior by their parents or coaches continues and the child gets sick of it, wanting to quit, parents usually say, "We started this and we are going to finish it; we're not quitters." When older kids are subjected to this poor behavior by adults, they often just tune them out, or many times will quit or display other rebellious behavior. If parents and coaches do not have the proper perspective about pressure, every strikeout, every error, every time a kid is thrown out stealing a base, will seem like a life-or-death situation to that kid. They'll be playing tight, not loose. They will not be having fun. It's all tied together. The next thing to go is their self-confidence. Once that's gone they will pretty much be "afraid to fail instead of expecting to succeed." We can help kids turn this around by taking a positive approach. Encouragement, and most of all, *patience,* are what are needed here. There are no substitutes for correct practice, correct teaching, and when developing a skill to a high level, correct repetitions.

Lots of correct repetitions!

Remember that reacting negatively towards kids, or umpires, for that matter, is shown in many ways, not just verbally. Throwing your hands up in the air, rolling the eyes, shaking your head, and kicking the dirt are all negative responses that ignorant people deny by saying "What are you talking about? I didn't say a word," when someone attempts to correct their unconstructive behavior. Kids pick up on these silent, but harmful behaviors by adults and it adds more pressure as they try harder to please arrogant coaches and overbearing parents, or sometimes just give up.

Thomas, a fourteen-year-old player on one of my teams, had this response when I asked him why he didn't steal second base after I had given him the sign in a perfect steal situation: "But, the catcher has a good arm; I was afraid I would get thrown out." Thomas, a very talented player, always played with fear—fear of his father's response if he failed. Consequently, he always played it safe. Constant pressure to succeed from his father took the joy out of baseball for Thomas. In another instance, Bill, a friend of mine and coach of his daughter's travel team of ten-year-olds, relayed to me one of the worst examples of behavior that I have heard of during a kid's game. Emily, after hitting the ball and getting on base, was given the sign to steal second base by her coach. She was thrown out by the catcher. When she got back to the dugout she was met by her mother who grabbed the face mask on her helmet and pushed her head back, hitting the dugout wall, and then jerked it forward while yelling "Don't do that again!" What kind of pressure do you think ten-year-old Emily will be under the next time she is asked to steal a base?

Play your role as a parent or coach by taking the pressure away when working with young players and not expecting instant success when learning new skills. Instead, make sure you are teaching correct technique and challenge them to improve over time.

It takes discipline and effort to train properly and consistently.

This truth is a really simple concept that anyone can understand, but many do not want to accept, because this correct approach to training can really get in the way of instant gratification *since it also takes time.* Muhammad Ali, perhaps the best boxer of all time, puts it this way: "The fight is won or lost far away from witnesses—behind the lines, in the gym, and out there on the road, long before I dance under those lights."

If Ali were to approach his training backwards, like so many young ballplayers do because their parents expect them to succeed before they have mastered the basics, he would not have become "The Greatest." A boxer knows all too well that if he goes into a fight unprepared for the level of competition he faces, he will likely be knocked out cold. This same principle applies to a young baseball player. If the training is not equal to the task (competition level), or if the training is weak, good results will be hard to find. What you will find is a feeling of pressure because you are not prepared. How can it feel like a challenge if you know you are obviously outmatched? *For it to feel like a challenge there needs to be hope.* You give yourself hope by developing the discipline to put forth a consistent good effort. You must challenge *yourself* first and realize that the real opponent is you. Only then will you have the awareness to feel challenged instead of pressured during competition. If you do nothing to help yourself reach your goals, you will always feel pressure. When you are unprepared for the level of competition you face, you will only get good results if the other, more skilled team, somehow has a bad day, falls apart, and plays down to your level. This hardly qualifies as success. You do not want to go through life hoping that others will fail so that you can experience success.

To make matters worse, in youth sports, many parents have not learned this lesson themselves or just let their emotions get the best of them. They are not playing their role as a parent very well. I often see these parents standing outside the fence by their son or daughter near the position that he or she is playing, basically badgering them the whole time. Now, not only is the player struggling because their training is insufficient, but the parent is adding more pressure and taking all the fun out of being on the baseball field. What a memory we are creating here! These parents must think that they can *talk* their child into having success at something for which their child has not properly trained. It won't happen! Remember, kids will play their best when they know that the adults around them are supportive, *whatever* happens.

Play your role as a parent by recognizing this truth: That putting pressure on a kid whose skills are undeveloped will not bring the results that you seek.

Playing baseball is very challenging and every practice, game, and season should be looked upon as steps along the way on your child's baseball journey. If you can do this, it will help you avoid being one of those overbearing parents who puts pressure on your kid during the game. You will gain the ability to stop expecting immediate success from your child and let them have fun, developing over time through correct training. You will begin to recognize your role as the one who encourages, motivates, and gives perspective to situations that your young player does not understand. Your mind will now be clear to see the real milestones as they happen, instead of pretending that your child has reached them.

Many parents have made this statement to me over the years: "I finally just decided to not go to my child's game because I couldn't control myself." What a shame! Where is the success in that? What is driving this level of emotion where you can't control yourself at your child's ballgame? I imagine you are taking the pressure off your child by not showing up, but you are also showing them a very poor example of how to deal with the realities of life when you can't even control yourself at a kid's game. You are running away from the truth. You have lost perspective and it's hurting your child's experience on the ball field and possibly in other areas of their life as well.

Make it your goal to understand the process of training and you will experience the joy that "being in the moment" creates when you watch your child play and develop as a player, instead of misery because you are so concerned about results or other people's success.

As adults, we have all experienced these two dynamics (pressure and challenge) in our own lives already. Remember times in your life when you felt pressure, maybe before a big test in college or on the job when you felt like you were in over your head a little bit. Not a good feeling, right? How did you deal with it? Did you just crumble under the pressure and accept failure? Were others around you helpful, or did they show disappointment in you because you couldn't "just do it?" How do you think a child feels after a failure when they see and hear nothing but disappointment from the adults in their presence? Most parents whose kids I have coached or taught have found some success at one thing or another. My guess is that they accepted the challenge and studied hard for that big test or were proactive at work and got more training and found a way to bring themselves up to par; making excuses was not an option. And if they think about it, there were people who encouraged them along the way. This is exactly how it should be when it comes to our kids and learning to play baseball. *There is plenty of pressure already, without parents adding more.*

Show your kids that you are not concerned about immediate results, but are more focused on their baseball journey and helping them to have fun, developing skill over time. Let them see how much you care whether they win or lose, whether they had a good day on the field or a bad day. If they have tried their best, and all they see is disappointment on your face, you have not fulfilled your role.

Kids need to know we support them whether they succeed or fail. If we constantly yell at kids when they fail, they will feel that they only have value to us when they are successful. They will be afraid to fail and will play tentatively because they don't want to disappoint their parents and coaches. This is the worst-case scenario for a young player. They will begin to make excuses for their failures and eventually want to quit, believing that it's easier to quit than it is to deal with their parents' unrealistic expectations. If we help kids learn to "embrace challenge" they will have fun and will learn to raise the bar themselves. They will develop self-respect, self-esteem, self-confidence, and self-discipline because they know we support them and are more concerned with their development over time (effort) instead of immediate results (outcome) that are out of balance with their current level of training and ability. They will feel challenged instead of pressured.

Chapter 11

Understand "What You Are Getting" Instead of "What You Are Not Getting"

A Parent's Role in Remembering What Has Been Achieved: teach kids to appreciate the opportunities they have gotten and not dwell on what others are getting.

If your natural instincts are to consistently notice "what you are not getting" instead of "what you are getting" in your life, you may be disappointed much of the time.

We become proficient at skills by building on what we have already learned. By being so concerned about what your child is not getting, you won't be able to help them build on what they have already learned because you won't see or appreciate it. All you will see is what your child didn't get and what someone else's child did. When a parent displays this kind of attitude in youth sports, it teaches the child how to manipulate the situation to get what they want, instead of putting forth the required effort to earn it. This is the recipe for remaining average or below as your child goes through their life wasting time seeking shortcuts. It will also affect how people perceive them. It is negative.

The path to excellence is narrow and you are off the path when you can only think about what you are not getting. If you want to achieve something that is difficult, get back on the path. Get to work and focus on your own effort, not other people's results. When parents and coaches teach this truth to young players, they are showing them the way, the way to get the most out of their ability. Make the choice to be one of those caring parents or coaches.

Remember that no situation is perfect. This is a good thing, because if things were always perfect, there would be no challenge. Without challenge there would be no purpose and we would not grow as people. We would simply exist. Our job is to step up to the challenges and use our God-given abilities to do the best that we can, building on what we have learned and not blaming others for what we didn't get.

Play your role as a parent by teaching your child to appreciate the opportunities they have gotten. Show your child that thanking a caring coach or instructor for their help is far more productive than blaming them when you don't get your way.

One of the biggest mistakes I have seen parents make is blaming the coach for their child's lack of progress. When this happens, what is more likely the cause of a child's lack of progress is this: parents are so concerned about what others are getting that their tendencies are to make excuses and place blame instead of channeling their energy in a more positive direction by helping their child develop skill and athleticism. Blaming coaches is very common in youth sports. Until parents gain some understanding about the process of developing skill, they are likely to make the mistake of expecting others to just make things happen for their child. They don't understand why another child is getting an opportunity that their child is not. They think that the coach is showing favoritism for that child. Sometimes this is the case, but more often than not, *opportunities exist because a player has been paying attention to his own effort and practicing the basics.* For people who understand this principle, it's easy to see why certain players are having success, natural ability or not.

Making a habit of complaining to the coach or others about issues such as another player playing a position that you think your child should be playing is counterproductive. A more positive approach would be educating yourself about the basic skills of baseball so that you can help your child understand what natural talents they have and build on them through proper training. *Forget about what others are doing and focus on what you are doing.* This approach leads somewhere good. As time passes, you will see results. You are no longer concerned about "what you are not getting" because you and your child are taking steps to improve yourselves and by doing so, you are creating change and new opportunities that will be ahead; you are winning. If you or your child are not willing to put in the time to practice, you should not expect much; your only responsible alternative is to stay off the coach's back, unless he is abusive. If he really is an abusive coach, it'll just be a matter of time until he cooks his own goose. Others will see it as well and action will be taken against him. Blaming a coach is convenient but is a poor approach to achieving excellence and leads nowhere except right back to the same place: complaining!

Blaming others becomes a weak substitute for what will really help your child, and it's what you will do when you only see "what you are not getting." If you stay with this approach, you are losing, and so is your child.

When parents' high expectations for their child are not met, it's easy to forget how much a caring coach or instructor has taught them the first time something doesn't go their (your) way. Emotions often overrule common sense when it comes to our kids. This can happen to anyone because it's a natural response to want to protect our children. By criticizing a good coach, your ego has convinced you to seek a feel-good result, and by doing so you are serving your own needs, not your child's. We all want the best for our kids but we should pay attention to *their* needs, not our own. What your child needs is to continue their training, building on what they have already learned, and developing their skill in spite of any coach who has denied them an opportunity for whatever reason. On any journey, there are obstacles to overcome. Do a little research on proper technique and take the time to help your child, or let an experienced instructor help your child with what they need to become a good ballplayer. You'll be pleased to find out that in time, your child will learn to overcome obstacles with good effort. If you have the patience to do this, soon it won't matter what that coach thought because your child will develop real skill and other opportunities will surface as the journey continues. If you do not have the patience to do this (develop skill and attitude) you are likely to place a time frame on the process of training. This outcome-oriented approach will put your child's progress in jeopardy because your need for immediate gratification will distract you from what will help your child develop sustainable skills: *time, effort, and correct attitude.*

I once had a parent at my martial arts school make this disrespectful statement to me when I explained that her kids were not quite ready for a high-level belt test. She said: "The training should have been better; they should be farther along by now." Not only was she professing to know more than me about my martial arts training (thirty-three years at that time), but she had taken for granted what her kids had already learned. Three years earlier they were very much uncoordinated and could barely do jumping jacks correctly. Now they are athletic, have developed great discipline and respect, and if they continue, will one day achieve what most students give up on: becoming a black belt. Her kids understand the process, but it remains to be seen if the mother can put aside her need for feel-good results based on her own emotional response. If not, it could eventually undermine all the hard work the kids have put in.

When it comes to developing skill and achieving goals, the same simple principles hold true, whether it's in martial arts, baseball or any sport or activity: giving a good effort will help you; making excuses will hurt you.

The path to excellence is long, winding, and very narrow. You won't find many people on it as you travel with your child through the process of becoming a good ballplayer, martial artist, musician, woodworker, or whatever your child's interest happens to be. Letting your emotions make decisions for you along the way will surely get you lost and off the path. Pay more attention to your intuition and you will have a clearer vision of where you are going. Many times we ignore our intuition (which is usually right) because it doesn't serve our immediate need for satisfaction. Our intuition tells us when something is working and to keep going until we achieve our goals. Our emotions tell us we want it right now; they tell our intuition to be silent. If your emotions win this battle, it's your child who will lose.

The parent I mentioned earlier who made the statement "the training should have been better; they should be farther along by now" had her kids at my gym an hour after that conversation. She was conflicted between emotions and intuition. The kids have been coming three times a week ever since, just like before the disrespectful conversation. This mother's intuition is to bring her kids to a place where they are learning valuable life lessons and are becoming excellent athletes in the process, but her emotions told her to speak up because other kids were getting ahead of hers. She emotionally spoke up and blamed the very person who had trained them from Day One to their current advanced status. Ironically, she got angry with me because I was treating her kids fairly. The problem was that she couldn't see it. Her emotions were telling her that the definition of fair was that her kids should be promoted because other kids had been promoted. Yet her intuition was telling her to continue to bring the kids for instruction because deep down she knew the training was correct, her kids had benefited greatly, and eventually they would reach their very distinguished goal of becoming a black belt in karate. Although this example happened in a martial arts school, the same principle applies on a baseball field: *control your emotions or they will control you.*

Fairness

Being fair doesn't mean that everyone gets the same thing every time. It doesn't mean that things are always going to be easy. There are different levels of ability, interest, and attitude that play a huge role in how fast someone progresses. Being fair *does* mean that you will be held accountable for poor effort or lack of respect. It also means that you will be complimented or rewarded only when you deserve it, and as it applies to serious training, when it is appropriate. When a coach or teacher is fair, recognize and be thankful for it, because rewarding your child for something they do not deserve is very unfair to them and will not help your child grow as a person.

Usually, there are very good reasons why things happen the way they do, but sometimes there *is* a situation that is very wrong or unfair. If this situation continues and you determine that it outweighs any benefits that you are receiving from the activity, you can always choose to stop participating and move on. Just remember that no situation is perfect. When a coach is unfair and it is obvious to everyone, don't let his negative behavior affect your child for the rest of their life by using the coach as an excuse. Think of him as an obstacle that you will overcome by helping your child refocus their efforts in a more positive way in spite of him. If you can do this, eventually you will realize that the coach had nothing to do with holding your child back. In fact, you may even thank him for waking you up to the fact that it is by your own efforts that opportunities will be created, not by blaming others.

Play your role as a parent by being the responsible person that you are, not by criticizing coaches because your child didn't get what others did. Make it about your child instead of yourself and you will see the correct path to take.

When I was young, I remember my mother always telling me to count to ten before reacting to a situation that upset me. That's some very good advice that we should all remember and make it our goal to achieve for the benefit of everyone involved. Letting the emotions subside and your mind get clear before reacting is a very responsible thing to do. Once again, look back and reflect on it. Realize what has been achieved. Do not take for granted or forget all the good things that have happened along the way and remember that it takes time and great effort to develop baseball skills or anything that is difficult. Leave your ego at home when you go to your child's ball game and you will see these things more clearly.

Reread the last paragraph and decide for yourself if this approach might be better than blaming others when your child doesn't get their way, or maybe, better put, doesn't get *your* way. One thing that I have become very aware of through my many years of coaching and teaching kids is this: how parents react to situations is crucial to their child's development as a player and a person.

Your child will be aware of your attitude, good or bad, and is likely to adopt it for themselves.

Dr. Gail Saltz, a psychiatrist and television commentator said this on the *Today Show* one morning: "What's wrong with today's kids is what's wrong with today's parents."

I think that there is some truth in that statement, but it doesn't have to apply to you. Make the choice to be different from many of today's parents and remain positive through your child's youth sports experience. If you do, you will see all the benefits you are receiving and whenever doubt arises you will take the high road instead of the low road.

The Big Picture

When you choose to focus on what you have gotten or are currently receiving from an activity, and especially if you look at it over a period of time, it can be easy to see the benefits. You will stop sweating the small stuff. You'll see how much you have benefited *even though things were not perfect.* If your expectations for your child are not being met, reconsider the things that are bothering you. Are they really affecting your child's progress to the point where it's not worth doing? Is the coach really unfair or are you just using him as an excuse for your child's lack of interest, ability, or effort because your own ego can't stand the truth? Talking to the coach in a respectful manner about the situation can help. Blaming the coach or refusing to accept a logical and experienced explanation from him is disrespectful and can only hurt your child's progress. You're not playing your role very well if you do this. Letting your emotions get the best of you will not help your child become a better baseball player.

If, overall, you like the program and are basically satisfied, have respect for the coach and be willing to not make a big deal out of certain things that you don't understand. If you lash out at the coach just to make yourself feel good for a few minutes, you will have gained nothing to benefit your child's future. You still will not understand and it's only a matter of time until you repeat the same poor behavior so that you can feel good again. This will not help your child become a better baseball player. What will help your child develop, and help you feel good in the long term, is for you to have the humility to want to learn what the coach or teacher knows concerning your child's development as a player. When you become aware of your child's real needs, you'll be their best asset and not someone who causes embarrassment by making excuses for them. When there is a concern, make sure that your attitude about the situation is one with a good perspective and not a vindictive attack against the coach. For example, if your kid is batting last in the line-up, before you make a big deal out of it by talking behind the coach's back or confronting him in anger, ask yourself these questions: Is the coach a reasonable person? Has he treated the kids fairly overall? In what other ways has he helped my child develop?

Remember, the goal is to help your child improve, not to make the coach look bad. There are many reasons why someone might be batting last in the line-up. If no one was willing to do it, then I guess that the team would have to forfeit an out and only bat with eight players instead of nine. But wait… now the eighth batter is the last one in the line-up. Is anyone willing to do it? If not, now we only have seven batters. As you can see, this is not a team approach. It's an "all about me" approach. If you are struggling with this sort of anxiety about your child's baseball experience, you can turn it around *immediately* by helping them focus on their personal efforts and not the efforts of the coach, or of anyone else, for that matter. When you take this path, you will start to see things for what they really are. You will become aware of whether or not your child is putting forth the required effort necessary to achieve the goal. You will begin to treat coaches and teachers with the proper respect while holding your child accountable for their own effort or lack of effort. You'll now be helping your child become a better baseball player by understanding what you are getting instead of what you are not getting.

During a recent season, in a competitive league, I remember a situation in which a father confronted my assistant coach on this very issue. At the beginning of the season, this man's son, Ryan, had expressed an interest in playing catcher. So, along with a few other kids who wanted to try the position of catcher, we started working with them on the fundamentals. They were all nine-years-old, and inexperienced. Ryan showed some natural ability and more importantly, *desire* to learn how to do it. He progressed more quickly than the others and became the everyday catcher. The other kids were backups at the position. They played more at other positions.

Ryan also worked hard on becoming a good hitter. So did the others. As it turns out, some of the other kids progressed a little more quickly in this area and, at this point in their lives, were more consistent than Ryan at hitting. When Ryan's dad confronted my assistant, he was angry that Ryan was hitting at the bottom of the line-up and decided to make an issue of it, showing no respect for the coaches who had helped Ryan become a very good catcher who was getting more playing time than any of the other catchers. What Ryan's dad failed to realize was this: Ryan is just starting his baseball journey. His good efforts in working on his hitting will show results over time. Ryan will one day be a very competent hitter if he sticks with it and his dad learns *his* role in helping him on his journey. Ryan's opportunities will come in time. His dad wanted those opportunities right then, before Ryan was ready. He was only seeing what Ryan was not getting instead of acknowledging and being thankful for what he was getting, or his response to the situation would have been different.

This example is one that happened in a very competitive league. In these leagues, players are recruited and teams develop year after year, much like in the big leagues. Parents should be aware that it takes time to develop a competitive team, and having an "effort over outcome" attitude will help them understand what they are getting instead of what they are not getting. Coaches must pay attention to getting players in the positions where they have the best chance for success, or the team will not be competitive. In the recreational leagues, there are more opportunities for coaches to let players try different positions and different spots in the batting order. This is a fundamental difference between the recreational league and the more competitive travel leagues. Before making the decision to play in a highly competitive travel league, it would be wise to make sure that your child and the team is well prepared for the competition because, if not, this is what will likely happen: The other teams will not make the same mistakes that you do. Your team will be uncompetitive and lose most of the games, and problems will develop with certain parents. When this happens, it can seem like a long season and when it ends, everyone is thankful that it's over. Even if the coaches are knowledgeable and are successful with helping players develop individual skills, it becomes impossible for parents to see the progress that their child is making toward becoming a better baseball player because they are getting their butts kicked every time they play and it doesn't feel good; it's not much fun.

Parents should be realistic about their child's ability and make sure that they are in a league wherein they have a chance to be at least competitive with the other players. Your child may be the lead-off hitter in the recreational league, but at the bottom of the line-up in a competitive league. Either way, try to recognize and appreciate the improvement that your child is making in all areas of the game. If your child's goal (not your goal for your child) is to play on a competitive level, such as on a travel team or high school team, help them understand that comparing themselves to others usually leads to criticizing and distracts them from their own effort. If you can do this, you will be fulfilling your role in your child's baseball journey, and doing your best to help them have fun and develop as a player and as a person.

There is a very disturbing trend happening in youth sports these days, which can be summed up in the following statement: "The more we get, the more we want and expect we are entitled to."

Your child is not necessarily entitled to anything when it comes to playing baseball, other than an opportunity to just be on a team. Their role on that team will depend on many variables. Good coaches try to place players in positions wherein they can experience some success based on their current level of ability and experience. For those who argue that their child won't get that experience unless they get to play a certain position in games, the answer is that "learning the basics takes place in practice, not in games." If those basics are not mastered first, they will experience failure in recreational ball games, not to mention total frustration to the point of wanting to quit if they are on a competitive travel team. Individual practice is where your child will get the necessary repetitions to develop muscle memory. When parents complain to coaches that their (unprepared) child is not getting the same opportunities as other players (seeing what you are not getting), they are basically saying they want to just skip the basics and go right to their goal (success.) They feel their child is entitled even though they have not earned it. This never works and it is sending the wrong message to the child. Now, not only is the kid failing at baseball, but the parent is teaching them how to fail in life. It is not a winning way. It's a losing way.

Remember, you can choose to increase your own effort at any time.

Personal effort is what will help your child achieve their goal, not the parent playing politics with the coach or sitting in the stands making negative comments about others. If you are comparing your results or outcomes with someone else's, it's usually a mistake. When you are overly concerned that someone else's child got to play a position where you thought your child should play, your perception will be that they now have some sort of advantage. This narrow thinking does not lead to your child getting better; it leads to you watching someone else's child get better. Maybe your child got what they deserved. If the other kid made it a bigger priority and practiced more and your child did not, everyone got what they deserved. (*Do what you have always done, and get what you have always gotten.*) Or maybe it's as simple as other kids developing physically before your child, or a coach's preference. You have no control over these things. When you focus on personal effort, these realities will seem less important and the future will determine your destiny, not your current coach or anyone else.

If you are only seeing what opportunity you did not get in today's game or practice, and are not willing to reflect on what opportunities you have gotten and how much you have benefited in the past, you are losing your focus. You're not looking at the big picture. This is one time that remembering the past can have a positive effect. It can serve as a reminder that you have come a long way in your personal development and help you to be thankful for those who have assisted you. You have the option to choose to realize what your child has gotten out of a situation and sometimes you will find that they have really come a long way and you will be pleased. Other times, the truth may reveal that your child has not put forth the effort and things aren't happening quite as fast as they could have if they had put forth more effort. You also may find out that their real interest lies elsewhere and no amount of encouragement on your part will convince them to try harder.

Play your role as a parent by teaching your child to have respect, instead of resentment, for a coach or instructor who has helped them, because you don't always get what you want, especially when you want it.

Don't make the mistake of criticizing the very person who has taught your child many things in the past. If you have been fortunate enough to have had a caring coach teach your child valuable skills in the game of baseball, for example, never forget it; be thankful. Not everyone gets that opportunity. Oftentimes, when a team is on a losing streak or a player is having personal struggles on the field, it's easy to blame the coach even though he may be the very person who has helped your child in many ways so far. This is very disrespectful and is confusing to your child. *Kids understand who has helped them and they also understand who is making excuses for them.* There can be many reasons why a team or individual player is struggling. Most likely, the reason is inexperience. When the competition starts, it's easy to forget how old the kids actually are. Because of our natural tendency to want to win, we suddenly expect the kids to be better than they really are. This is very common these days, but when we expect too much too soon from kids, all kinds of problems will arise. Our own desire for our kids to succeed outweighs proper perspective and we blame someone like an umpire or a coach when our child experiences failure. Consider this: If your child is inexperienced, give him proper instruction and time to develop. If your child is experienced, but not doing as well as others, maybe he has slacked off in his training and a teammate with similar or sometimes less ability has increased theirs. If you are honest with yourself, it can be easy to see why the teammate received an opportunity where your child did not. Your child made it easy for them. In a competitive environment, your kid let down his efforts, maybe feeling that he had things locked up. If this is the case, he is now showing a lack of humility.

Very often, a lack of humility is more of a problem for the parent of a young athlete. Some parents cannot stand the fact that another kid has gotten something that their kid has not. I have noticed that young athletes themselves know where they stand in relation to their peers. If left up to them, a team would form just the way it should. Without outside influences from adults, kids will often make the correct decisions when it comes to who should play where on a baseball team, for example. They *know* whether or not they have put in the time to be the best pitcher, catcher, infielder, outfielder, etc. They also know who has put in the time to become a proficient hitter and who has not.

Where things get messed up is when coaches, parents, or other adults get involved in the wrong way, influencing the situation negatively. Sometimes coaches are weak and will give certain players special treatment over others after being influenced by an overbearing parent who just has to see their kid succeed right now. If this happens and you are the player on the short end of the stick, it might be a good time to remember what you are getting or have gotten that has benefited you so far in your career. Don't make excuses that will only get you lost and off the path of correct training. Continue to build on what you have already learned and focus on your own efforts. Remember your personal goals and realize that, when people get special treatment that maybe they didn't deserve or earn, they really haven't gotten much at all. *When other people are just making things happen for you without you putting forth the effort, it's a temporary situation at best, because time passes and, at some point, you will have to do it on your own.*

This is where the ones who have kept a good perspective and understood what they are getting out of a situation instead of what they are not getting will come into their own. Others, who have relied on getting special treatment from their parents and coaches, will fall behind. Good effort and perspective will win every time, eventually. Just be patient and understand what you are getting instead of what you are not getting.

Chapter 12

Dealing with Failure, Preparing for Success

A Parent's Role in Helping Kids Deal with Failure: when kids fail, consider it a teaching moment, not a preaching moment.

No one becomes successful without experiencing a certain amount of failure. When you are constantly making excuses for your child after they fail, instead of teaching them the value of overcoming failure with good effort, you will reap what you sow. Your child will likely follow your example, good or bad. Which way do you want it?

Making excuses is much easier and it's what most kids will do unless *taught* to do otherwise. When you experience a failure, it's what you do next that counts. If you learn to accept the fact that some failure—not that you *are* a failure—is normal as you pursue becoming excellent at something, you will let it go fast and stay focused on your immediate effort, which is something over which you have control. If you pay too much attention to the failure and dwell on it, instead of just learning from it and moving on, your chances of repeating the cause of the failure are high.

For example, when trying to hit a baseball, if your child is turning his head when he swings, he may be striking out a lot because he can't see the ball. If he does manage to hit the ball, but is falling off balance as his head turns, causing his eyes to look toward left field, he probably just got lucky. Getting lucky absolutely will not work when he gets older and the pitching is better.

When coaches and parents have no clue how to properly teach a skill like hitting, failure gets the spotlight because correct instruction is absent. All the kids are left with is the failure and no solution. Once the game starts, the pressure is on for kids, even if they haven't learned the techniques and they will be hoping to get lucky. There is not much success in getting lucky because luck cannot be sustained. Repeating correct mechanics is sustainable and a successful approach. *If no one takes the time to teach kids this skill by getting their head down as they swing so they can see the ball all the way in, they will continue to strike out and eventually just feel like a failure.* Add to that the fact that result-oriented adults may be making matters worse by yelling, and these unprepared kids have no chance at all.

Many people become coaches because they know something about the game of baseball. Some become coaches because they enjoy working with kids and they are good at it. Certain people are blessed with both of these assets. Whatever team your child is on, it's the parent's perspective and attitude that will the make the difference as to whether or not the experience is a positive one. Recognize and respect a coach's assets and your child will have a good experience. If your child is on a team wherein the coach does not know correct baseball techniques himself, don't waste your time blaming the coach for your child's failures; it doesn't lead anywhere. Become proactive by seeking private instruction from a knowledgeable teacher or *take the time* to learn these simple techniques yourself. With the heightened level of competition in youth sports these days, there are many good books and videos available that teach the correct mechanics. By adopting a positive and humble attitude, parents can become the greatest asset their child has. You will recognize a good and experienced coach when you see one and you will trust his efforts to help your child become a better ballplayer. You will also realize that an inadequate coach is temporary, but your efforts to help your child are a permanent endeavor.

Instead of making excuses for your kids, raise your level of awareness about what it takes to play the game of baseball successfully. Just remember that success doesn't mean becoming a Major League Baseball player, although it is considered the highest achievement that a player can attain. Success happens at every step of the journey when you are putting forth a good effort to compete at your current level and building skills to compete at the next level. Teaching your kids to achieve success by getting the most out of their ability, one step at a time, will lead to life-changing results. They will develop an awareness that real success is focusing on their own effort instead of comparing themselves to others. Some players do make the major leagues. Natural ability must be there, but perseverance, sacrifice, commitment, patience, endurance, and most of all, *passion* are the ingredients that are present in the recipe for success at the highest levels. The professional athletes who also have humility and a good attitude are the best examples in whatever sport they play. This is also true in youth sports for parents and young athletes.

Yelling at kids during the game to keep their head down when they swing or any other techniques that are not yet learned is wasting your breath. Because we have emotions, it's something that will probably always happen, but you can choose to be different. If you do, your child will benefit greatly. Technique needs to be taught and learned at practice. During the game, if you expect more from kids than they are capable of, you are adding pressure and setting them up for failure. I have seen kids give up and aimlessly wave the bat at the ball three times so they can just get it over with and go sit down in the dugout. They are obviously not having fun, but it doesn't have to be that way. First of all, coaches and parents have to realize how difficult it is to hit a baseball, and second, they should acquire some basic knowledge themselves and be willing to take the time to teach it. When parents expect kids to perform a difficult skill like hitting a baseball without first letting them learn how to do it through proper instruction, it's the parents who have failed. If your child is struggling with learning how to hit a baseball, try this simple experiment which may help you appreciate what they are experiencing: Pick up a bat and ask a coach or a friend to throw some pitches for you to try and hit, and do it in front of other people.

Often, young ballplayers are at a disadvantage because they are trying to live up to their parent's or coach's unrealistic expectations. When they are unable to meet those expectations, they feel like a failure; they feel like they have let people down. If this trend continues, kids will develop a fear of failure. Now you've got a problem. This can lead to low self-esteem and complete lack of confidence.

We should teach kids to play like they expect to succeed, instead of being afraid to fail.

The only way this works is as follows: *Adults need to keep a positive attitude and show encouragement instead of disappointment when things are not going as planned.* Kids will respond in a positive way when the adults around them have a good perspective. Confidence will grow because they know their parents and coaches support their efforts and are not overly concerned about outcomes. They will expect success because they need not worry about failure. Keeping a good perspective will go a long way in helping you help your kids become good ballplayers.

Play your role as a parent or coach and remember how young your players are and realize that they do not have to become superstars overnight; in fact, they don't have to become superstars at all.

Sometimes the best medicine after *consistently* experiencing failure is more practice and sometimes it's just taking a break. Practice builds confidence; taking a break can bring back desire. It's all relative to the situation and the person. Paying attention to your child's emotional needs as a baseball player is equally important as paying attention to his physical needs. But to ignore the truth of the situation by thinking that things will be better next time without any additional effort, either mentally or physically or both, is a fairytale. If a player is normally confident and just has a bad day, that's different. He will probably just forget it, unless his parents choose to make a big deal of it. Sometimes, when my son Phillip would have a bad game, all I would say is "Let's go get a milkshake."

Baseball is a great game to learn how to deal with failure because it happens during the whole game.

Some players develop the bad habit of making excuses when they fail. Many times they learn this from their parents who can't stand to see their kids experience failure. Making excuses for your kids when they fail, instead of teaching them accountability, will show them how to give in to failure instead of teaching them how to succeed. Making excuses is an attempt to take the easy route. This will not work in baseball and it will not work in life. When you strike out or make an error, your ability to put it behind you will be directly tied to your mental and physical preparation up to that point. *If you have not put in the time to develop the skill required to have good at-bats or play consistent defense, you will not have the confidence to know if you can trust your efforts during the game, and often, failure is the result.* Here come the excuses: It must be the umpire, or the lousy weather; nobody can field a ball on this infield, etc. If whoever is coaching the team does not understand how to deal with this by teaching kids good preparation and perspective, or certain parents have their own agenda, everyone is in for a miserable season.

We all understand that when failure happens, there is a reason. But what is it? Here is where we see the difference in people. Some are preparing themselves for eventual success because they see the real reason for the failure and are willing to deal with it. They know that by being consistent in their training, they will be well prepared and minimize their chances of failure. When failure happens, they realize that it's just part of the process and they don't make excuses. They have experienced some success because they are patiently taking one step at a time on the road towards excellence.

Others have not trained hard or prepared well for whatever reason, yet expect the same results as the person who has. They are going to experience failure often if this thinking continues. Their skill level and the difficulty of the task will be out of balance. This is where you see people looking for the "quick fix" or the magic technique. Maybe getting the latest "great bat" will help. *Remember that there is no substitute for correct repetitions.* The fact of the matter is that if you are not willing to put in the time and effort, you should not expect much.

Failure is something that happens to everyone; even the most talented and gifted people experience failure. How we perceive this in young athletes is important. It's more important than the game itself. If your talented eight-year-old strikes out and his reaction is to start crying, how do you deal with it? I have seen dads so embarrassed by this that they will grab the kid in front of everyone and shake him while exclaiming "There's no crying in baseball! And if you don't stop, or do it again, we are going home!" Maybe all the kid needed was a quick hug and a little encouragement. It's simple. Cut him some slack. He's eight-years-old! Maybe he started crying because, even at eight, he is well aware of his dad's expectations of him to be successful right now. Possibly, he has become afraid to fail. He hears a coach's or his parent's negative tone when he makes mistakes instead of positive reinforcement, and he's not emotionally prepared to handle it. If he's still crying at eighteen maybe we have a problem, but I doubt that will be the case, because either he will have gotten sick of people's unrealistic expectations, rebelled, and quit playing baseball, or the overbearing dad will have seen the consequences of his own poor attitude and made an effort to change. If the latter is true, the eight-year-old will have been afforded the opportunity to progress at a normal rate and everything should work out.

If parents and coaches stay positive with young players at all times, even when correcting undesirable behavior, the kids will benefit more than if parents and coaches react negatively and just yell at them. When kids experience failure, this is our opportunity to teach them how to deal with it. This is a lesson that is well worth learning at a young age. If we do not teach them ourselves, kids will decide for themselves how to deal with it. Many times I have witnessed kids stop trying to make difficult plays because the chance for failure is greater. They become afraid to take a chance on anything that could cause them to experience failure. They become underachievers because it's safer. If parents and coaches are not playing their role correctly, that's what can happen. How can you blame a kid for taking the safe route if he always gets a negative response when he doesn't succeed? He has been taught at an early age to be afraid to fail. When you are driven by fear, it's almost impossible to develop confidence as a baseball player. Skill development will be slow because you refuse to risk failure.

You can't experience success without experiencing failure; the more difficult the task, the more likely failure will precede success.

By learning to self-motivate, you will minimize your chance of failure, and in time you will come to trust this truth as you realize that you are never disappointed that you talked yourself into doing something positive for yourself or others. You will never say, "I wish I wouldn't have helped that person who was struggling; what was I thinking?" Or, "I'm sorry that I talked myself into working out today." Instead, you will feel good about yourself and be glad that you were able to put forth a positive effort. It works every time.

You are never sorry when you self-motivate, but doing it consistently is easier said than done. Keeping your goal in mind can help. Visualize seeing yourself as the successful person you want to be and motivate yourself to take one more step today toward that goal. If you do this, you are being successful. If you are unable to motivate yourself, you are more likely to take the easy way out, which is to do nothing at all or to make excuses. The unfortunate result of this lack of self-motivation is that you will learn to accept that *you* are a failure.

The more you self-motivate, the sooner it will lead to better self-discipline, resulting in better preparation. Eventually, it will become automatic. In other words, you will be setting yourself up for success instead of failure. Learning to self-motivate is something that needs to be learned at a young age because, if it's not, making excuses will become your reality. Making excuses can become a nasty habit and hard to overcome because you start to believe the excuses and blame others for your failures. For example, if you and another player are competing for the same position and the other player gets it, how will you react? If you are a self-motivator, you will realize you were prepared, but there were other dynamics in play that you had no control over. You will realize you failed to get the position, but you will not see yourself as a failure. *Self-motivators are always moving forward.* If you have not learned to self-motivate, you will see yourself as a failure or your ego will come to your defense, making excuses or blaming others. You will be moving backwards instead of forward. Once your ego takes control, you are out of control.

No one makes you fail. You make yourself fail by failing to take action when action is required; that's failure.

Play your role as a parent by teaching your child the value of self-motivation instead of making excuses for them when they lack effort.

When parents interrupt the learning process by trying to protect their child from failure, they are unwittingly handing it to them on a silver platter. Their kids will never learn the valuable lesson of dealing with failure because their parents won't allow it to happen. Just like life itself, baseball presents constant challenges, and some of those challenges will end up being failures. But we must move forward and challenge ourselves anyway. If we never challenge ourselves, we will not grow, so we must learn to risk failure. The only way we will ever risk failure is if we feel we have a good chance for success. The only way we will be confident that we have a good chance for success is if we have prepared for success.

Preparation reduces the risk of failure.

I have heard people say "Failure is not an option!" What does that mean? That you will do anything or hurt anyone so you can succeed? If you are a real winner, that is not an option! People who make these statements do not realize that failure is a possibility. Because of this arrogant attitude they will lack the humility to learn all they can so they can minimize their chances of failure. They become willing to do anything; they will win at all costs. People who gain success at the expense of another's wellbeing or reputation are ultimate losers. Their success is not sustainable and when they fall, they will fall hard.

If you want failure to not be an option, let your excellent effort do the talking!

This is a winning way.

Chapter 13

Master the Basics before Attempting the Advanced

A Parent's Role in their Child's Skill Development: keep the fun in it as your child develops technique, one step at a time.

Pick up your front foot and stride toward the pitcher; move your hands back into loaded position before you swing; hit the ball to the opposite field on the outside pitch; *pull* the ball on the inside pitch; hit the ball up the middle on the pitch down the middle of the plate. The coach is barking out these instructions to his players throughout the practice and it's all very good and correct information. The problem is that the players are nine and ten-years-old and can't even achieve balance on a consistent basis, giving them little chance to accomplish these very good, very correct, and very *advanced* techniques.

First Things First
It's very common in youth baseball to see coaches and parents skipping the basics and trying to teach advanced techniques

and concepts to kids who haven't even figured out their batting stance yet and are still turning their heads when they swing. Because they are turning their heads and their stance is inconsistent, these inexperienced kids are not seeing the ball well, their balance is poor, and they will struggle to hit the ball no matter what parents and coaches want.

The results of this backwards approach are predictable: *Frustration*, not only for the kids who are constantly failing to hit the ball, but also for the parents and coaches whose unrealistic expectations are not being met.

Doesn't sound like much fun, does it?

When kids sign up for baseball, the main goal, of course, is to have fun. Having fun should not come at the expense of learning sustainable skills, however. If basics are taught correctly to all players, having fun will be the result because success will be easier to achieve. Success doesn't always mean winning the game. For some kids, it may mean just making contact with the ball. Once basics are mastered, more advanced skills will be easier to teach and learn. Kids may have several coaches during their playing years. Early on, if they get a coach with a weak foundation in teaching baseball skills, they are likely to pick up bad habits that will have to be overcome in the future if they hope to continue to higher levels of play.

When you teach advanced technique to players before they are proficient at the basics, the results are always weak and disappointing. The ultimate result of having fun will be hard to achieve.

It's not much fun striking out all the time but it doesn't have to be so. Teach a six-year-old kid to keep their head still and their forehead coming down as the ball approaches the bat and chances are that they will have some success because they can see the ball. A very effective way to do this with young kids is the "Ike to Mike" drill. For a right-handed batter, his chin will start at his left shoulder which we will call "Ike." As the ball approaches the hitting zone and he begins his swing, his chin will end up at his right shoulder which we will call "Mike." This will bring the head down and the eyes to the ball as it hits the bat. Now, instead of swinging out of his shoes and losing balance because his head went flying out—taking his eyes off of the ball—he will have better balance because his energy is more focused where it should be: on the ball. By just repeating the concept of balance—weight on the balls of the feet, not the heels—and the Ike to Mike drill, a young, inexperienced hitter will have all he needs for quite a while. It will build confidence instead of failure.

After he has mastered this basic technique, he will be ready for the rest of the hitting mechanics to be taught, but not before. *The biggest challenge is for the adults to be patient enough to let the basic technique take hold and become an automatic reaction.* When you move on to advanced technique too soon, it's like building a house with a weak foundation. You can make it look like a house and it will stand for a while, but there will be problems in the future. Its initial appearance and stability are not sustainable.

Many inexperienced coaches teach techniques that they *think* are right, not what they *know* to be correct based on their thorough research on the subject.

"Get your back elbow up!" This is one you hear at youth baseball parks all the time from parents and coaches who *think* that this is the correct information. What this does for a kid with little or no training is make the task even harder by adding an extra step. The elbow now has to come down close to the body to achieve maximum leverage while swinging the bat. Why not just start there? "Get the bat off your shoulder!" When a young player hears this, the bat comes off the shoulder all right. Usually by about a foot! Now his swing is likely to be long and slow instead of short and quick. Because the swing is long and slow, the player will feel the need to start the swing too soon in order to get the bat around in time to make contact with the ball. Keeping the hands closer to the body will allow a player to be short and quick; he will be able to wait longer before he swings, thereby letting him see the ball longer before he commits, making it easier to tell the location of the ball. An easy way to demonstrate quickness is to take a pencil

"One Point" Balance Drill

This is a balance drill I use while teaching martial arts, which also works well for baseball players. It teaches us an awareness of the balance point of the body, which is two fingers below the naval, also known as the "one point" in martial arts.

Start with your feet shoulder-width apart, head centered over the belly button. Keep your head still and consciously locate your energy in the lower abdomen. Bring the knee to the chest and hold with both hands clasped together for a count of ten. At first, you will probably sway like a tall tree in the wind. Your head will go off-center and you will lose balance. Before giving in and dropping your foot to the floor, consciously bring the head back to being centered over the "one point" while staying calm and breathing easily. You will become still; you will be balanced.

Once you have mastered this, transition to the second position, which is to bring the heel of your foot to the buttocks without putting your foot down. Reach back and grab your ankle with both hands and hold for a count of ten.

As you do this, your mental focus should be on keeping the head still and centered over the naval, energy located in the lower abdomen. In time, with a steady mind, your body will memorize this feeling of balance; it will feel normal.

and draw a large circle. This circle represents the hands casting out from the body. Now draw a small circle. This circle represents the hands staying close to the body. Which one takes longer to complete?

Remember, when you see a big leaguer holding his hands far away from his body, you are not watching a beginner. Some big-league players keep their hands in close; some do not. At their very advanced stage, it's a matter of preference. Along with having great strength, these players have developed a keen sense of rhythm and timing by perfecting the basic techniques years before you are seeing them, and as a result, they have developed their own unique hitting style that works for them. When kids mimic major-league players it doesn't always work out if their favorite player happens to be someone with an unorthodox hitting style. There are several big-leaguers, however, who have maintained a very basic approach to hitting, and these players are a very good example for a young player to watch. Be aware of this while watching a major-league game on television and it will be a very useful learning tool. Many times, after getting a hit, the swing will be played back in slow motion and the commentators will describe the mechanics as they are happening. The point is there is a lot to know and learn about teaching basic mechanics to young, inexperienced players. It's not rocket science, though, and most people are capable of doing it. *You just have to care and be patient.* You also have to put aside any need for instant results based on your unrealistic expectations and let your child perfect the basics one step at a time.

Results need to be measured with proper perspective. A good result for a six or seven-year-old kid during their first lessons would be an increased awareness of good balance whether they hit the ball or not. Achieving good balance should be a top priority. Without it, even basic technique will be difficult and becoming consistent will only be a dream. Like all other aspects of sports, it must be practiced. Just telling a kid to have balance without giving them proper instruction as to how to do it will lead to the same place every time—lack of balance. Kids as young as six or seven-years-old who do not have a natural sense of balance are often overlooked by self-serving coaches who want results now and will not take the time to teach this very fundamental technique. Instead, they will let the kids with more natural athletic ability have more playing time. They do this because it's the easy way; yes, it's the easy way to win, but at what cost?

Play your role as a parent or coach by learning techniques that will help your young players achieve better balance, and take the time to teach it to them.

Learning the proper basics yourself is how you become a *coach* instead of being a babysitter.

There are many good books and videos that show the basics and how to teach them. Cal Ripken Jr.'s *Coaching Youth Baseball the Ripken Way* is one of them. It shows what *mastering the basics* means for kids and is age-appropriate. It also has a lot of good information for parents on what it means to master the basics of coaching. Anyone who takes on the responsibility of coaching should arm themselves with as much knowledge as possible. It's a huge responsibility.

These days, we have a lot of access to viewing professional baseball players. The internet, the MLB Network, and ESPN provide us with as much as we can handle, so we are constantly soaking in the best players in the world, making even the most difficult plays look easy. It's important to watch these players, because it shows us where good preparation and perfect practice can lead. It doesn't *always* lead to becoming a professional player, but it definitely leads to getting the most out of your ability.

When we watch professionals, we are seeing the *results* of a long journey. We are seeing all those basic drills and correct repetitions that brought them there, although these basics are sometimes masked by more advanced technique. Many times, inexperienced coaches at the youth level teach advanced skills too soon based on what they see the pros do. To the inexperienced eye, it may be hard to see what is actually happening when a big leaguer swings the bat or turns that sweet double play. Hidden in those beautiful swings and solid defense we see are all the very basic techniques we should teach young players. The trick is to teach these basics in the proper sequence, building the swing and fielding mechanics one step at a time. When you start skipping steps because you are impatient or are unsure of the steps yourself, *the young player's progress will suffer.*

There are many ways for parents and coaches to learn the basics. You just have to be open to learning and then you will become aware of the many opportunities. While visiting my home state of Minnesota, I watched a Twins game on television one evening. When the game was over, the broadcasters, some of them former professional baseball players, held a brief clinic on the basics. This night, they were showing the basics of bunting. If any parent or coach of a young player were watching, they would have seen exactly how to teach a young player to execute a bunt properly. The Twins showcase a different technique after each game for their viewers to watch and learn. This is a great learning tool for coaches and parents who just finished watching professionals make it look easy. It looks easy for the big-leaguers because the basics have become automatic. When a "smokin' hot" ground ball has been hit to a player and he reacts in a split second to make a great play, it looks pretty amazing!

Play your role as a parent by teaching your young ballplayer that, to make amazing plays, they must practice the basics until they become automatic reactions.

When it comes to hitting a baseball, a young player must have an understanding that it's what they do before they swing that counts.

Good preparation is crucial.

An example of good preparation for a young player would be to first establish a balanced stance. When hitting off a batting tee, for example, if a player does not start from the same balanced stance every time, they cannot expect the same result every time. The first goal when working on tee drills should be making good contact with the ball consistently. It's just sitting there. The only thing that can change is the player's swing mechanics.

Here is an example of basic preparation before swinging: Placing the feet a little wider than shoulder-width apart is a good place to start. A knowledgeable parent or coach can help adjust from there. Next, bend slightly at the waist and knees and reach across to touch the outside of the plate with the bat. This will shift the weight off the heels to the balls of the feet and also ensure good plate coverage while maintaining a relaxed posture. Now, bring the hands close to the shoulder as you take a breath. Breathing will relax the shoulders and focus the mind. Next, shift about 60% of your weight to the back leg. This preparation should be taught to a young player until it is muscle memory and it is exactly what a big-leaguer would do, although many of them have developed unorthodox ways to prepare that work for them.

By repeating this process exactly every time without fail, the big-leaguer is preparing himself mentally and physically to execute the excellent swing mechanics that have become automatic through years of correct training. By *practicing* this initial preparation until it becomes automatic, the young, inexperienced player is preparing himself to more easily learn the next part of the swing mechanics until they *also* become automatic.

Play your role as a parent or coach by teaching young players that wanting to hit the ball is not enough. It is their good preparation that will help them achieve their goal of success.

Without this guidance, kids will swing without preparing, whether you pitch them one ball or one hundred balls. All they know is that they want to hit the ball; what they don't know is how to do it. Many kids are so anxious to swing the bat that when you put the ball on the tee they will swing before you are out of the way and take your head off if you're not paying attention. *They are prepared to swing without preparation.* Once good preparation has become automatic, a kid will have better success with learning the basic hitting mechanics. A coach or parent will now be able to effectively teach a player to load the hands, stride, and drive the ball with a quick swing because the player's preparation is the same every time. If you attempt to teach any kind of hitting mechanics before kids master the very basic concept of good preparation, all you will get is frustration because of an inconsistent, weak foundation. *If the preparation is different every time, the result will be different every time.* As a young, inexperienced player progresses to becoming an older, more advanced player, natural tendencies and abilities, timing mechanisms, and increased strength play a part in the formation of an individual's technique.

Professional baseball players make routine plays look easy. When kids are just starting their baseball journey, those same routine plays appear almost impossible to accomplish. Big-leaguers have mastered the basics; kids have not. While we expect the professionals to make those plays every time, we can't expect the same from kids. If we do, we will add pressure that they are emotionally not prepared to handle. Going through the correct motions sounds easy, but there is a lot more to throwing, hitting and catching than meets the eye. For the advanced player, such as a professional, these motions have become part of them; they feel normal. They are now performing the basics in a masterful way. Depending on natural ability, maturity, and interest level, a young player may find these motions easy or difficult to master. What we can learn from this is that repetition of the correct, very basic motions helps us to achieve success on routine plays. Often, however, it's the adults in their lives who will make the difference as to whether or not a kid will have ultimate success. Will there be pressure to learn advanced technique too soon, or will there be *patience* to allow a young player to develop over time, mastering the basics first?

One of the biggest problems in youth baseball is when adults expect kids to do more than they are capable of. These types of adults are right on track to becoming a "win at any cost" parent or coach, resorting to anything they think will bring them immediate success. For these adults, whether or not it has anything to do with teaching proper mechanics or strategies that will help kids in the future is irrelevant. Their attitude is obvious: we must win today!

Lack of patience, lack of knowledge and experience, and lack of humility are usually present when basic instruction is absent.

Play your role as a parent or coach by teaching basics to all players on a consistent basis so that they will be prepared to play their role during the game. When you ask too much too soon from a young player, you are basically asking them to do the impossible. If their muscles have not been trained to perform the basic techniques on automatic, the advanced techniques will be overwhelming to them. If this unrealistic approach continues, the fun will be taken out of it and all that will be accomplished is the player deciding to quit.

On a baseball team, there are always different levels of talent and maturity. Some players have a lot of talent, but have not yet grown into it. While kids are still growing, their bodies may inhibit them from performing the technique easily if they are small for their age or may be growing so fast they can't control their movements. This is why it takes so much patience and awareness to be a good coach. Even if you know the advanced techniques, you must be patient and aware enough to teach them at the right time. *You can't practice the basics too much.* When basic technique is practiced on a regular basis, all the players will benefit by getting the most out of their ability. The player with natural ability will get even better, preparing himself for a higher level of competition, while the struggling player will have the opportunity to realize some success on a basic level, which will lead to more self-confidence.

The better you are at the basics, the better you will be at the advanced skills.

This is common wisdom in martial arts and it applies to baseball as well. In both disciplines, however, it's the teacher who will make the difference. In martial arts training, basic technique is constantly practiced even though a student may know, and be good at, advanced techniques. This is the path that leads to becoming a black belt, a mark of excellence in the martial arts. In baseball, it's common to see players *hoping* for success by using the same flawed technique over and over. Remember that you will not excel by accident; it takes effort. When the difficulty of mastering baseball skills is underestimated, it's a path that leads to a player eventually quitting because achieving excellence seems impossible to them, and they are right.

Hoping for success and expecting success are two very different dynamics: Those who are hoping for success have not trained; those who expect success *have* trained.

For centuries, martial arts training has set a good example for the process of achieving one's full potential. The opponent is really oneself. By learning to overcome in their personality such things as lack of humility, lack of confidence and self-esteem, the need for instant gratification, and disrespect for others, a martial arts student progresses through the ranks one step at a time, developing skills by accepting criticism from others who are more knowledgeable than themselves. The results are self-confident students who expect success and are *being* successful by preparing themselves through proper training.

On the ball field, when humility, patience, and respect are combined with teaching basic physical technique, the results are rewarding. The problem in baseball is that there is a game to win and many coaches have not mastered these moral principles and basic techniques themselves. When this is the case, the kids are left with leaders who take them down the wrong path. Winning becomes more important than development of players and, when that happens, progress in the way of developing sustainable skills is left to chance.

Pitching Basics

When young pitchers have issues such as sore elbows and shoulders, fatigue is probably at the root of it. Improper mechanics is a problem as well. Many times I have heard coaches say "It's okay to let kids throw curveballs; just teach them the proper way to do it."

It may be true that pitchers with proper mechanics are at no greater risk throwing a curve than a fastball, but assuming that a young, immature pitcher has developed the self-discipline to stick to a correct training regimen is not realistic. The problem is that these coaches do not understand this truth: it takes time to really learn technique. Just showing someone how to do something will not produce the desired results, unless the discipline to train correctly is also present. When competition begins, this truth can disappear really quickly, because the desired results are to strike the batter out with a curveball, whether it's thrown correctly or not! The desired result in today's society is that we win the game, not that we develop the discipline to train kids properly for the future.

If it means throwing curveballs before kids are physically ready to do so, the "win at any cost" coach will find a way to rationalize it in his own mind or just put it out of his mind completely in order to win the game. This is not a "master the basics before attempting the advanced" approach. When young pitchers are successful, whether they are throwing curveballs or not, they are at risk of being overused by selfish, win-at-any-cost coaches who lack perspective. Fatigue sets in, mechanics break down, and young pitchers are left with the consequences. In his book, *Any Given Monday*, Dr James Andrews, an orthopedic surgeon and sports medicine pioneer, states that "Every year more than 3.5 million children will require medical treatment for sports-related injuries, the majority of which are avoidable through proper training and awareness."

There are indeed negative consequences for kids who are unfortunate enough to have parents or coaches who let them throw curveballs before they are physically ready to do so. If they are having success, they get overused. They may have a great Little League Career, but their future in the game will be very uncertain because their elbows may not be able to withstand the strain that throwing a curve with improper mechanics can produce. To make matters worse, many kids learn how to throw the curveball from their fellow teammates, who are ill prepared to be teaching proper pitching mechanics.

There are exceptions to every rule, but the reason that the curveball is so effective in youth baseball is most likely this: The kids on the other team have not mastered the basics of hitting. It's usually not because the kid throwing the curveball has mastered the basics of pitching. For the inexperienced hitter, just seeing a curveball throws them off. What you usually see is the batter jumping back when he sees the curve, or just wildly swinging, hoping to get lucky. The win-at-any-cost coach will be thinking, "Why not throw him a couple more curveballs and strike him out?" When a young player falls in love with the curveball, his pitching career will suffer. Being able to locate the fastball should be Goal Number One!

In summary, when a pitcher who has mastered the basics of throwing a good fastball for strikes, is facing a batter with good hitting mechanics, the curveball is effective because it is an off-speed pitch which throws the batter's timing off. In contrast, when a pitcher who has not mastered the basics of throwing a good fastball is facing a hitter who has not mastered the basic hitting mechanics, the curveball only works for the pitcher because it causes fear in the batter: fear of being hit by a ball that is coming at him and then curves away.

In the first years of kid pitch, nine and ten-year-old ball, the need for basic training couldn't be clearer. If the pitchers can't get the ball over the plate, it affects the whole game. It becomes a very slow, boring game with one walk after another. Parents, players, coaches, umpires, and most of all, the young unprepared pitchers are not going to have as much fun as they could have. Let's start with the pitchers: Most kids, who say they want to pitch, take the mound with little or no training; however, the same pressure to throw strikes is there for them as it is for a trained pitcher. This is because in our society we are in love with winning. There is nothing wrong with wanting to win; there is everything wrong with putting pressure on young players who are completely untrained.

Because they can't get the ball over the plate consistently, they are in for a miserable experience. These untrained kids will feel the pressure from the crowd and their coaches; their teammate's demeanor toward them is usually more understanding. It's amazing to me that in this age of heightened competition, there isn't more awareness on the part of parents, coaches, and local recreation leagues to make sure that a nine-year-old pitcher gets some basic instruction before he is allowed to take the mound in a game. One or two lessons a few weeks before the season starts is not what I'm talking about. Some consistent training on the basics of pitching as an eight-year-old will go a long way toward achieving success next year as a nine-year-old. The training will have a chance to accumulate and become automatic.

Pitcher is the most pressure-filled position on the baseball field and it isn't fair to put a kid on the mound if they haven't practiced enough to gain some confidence. Most of the kids who attempt pitching for the first time have no training and can't do it; the results are disappointing. An additional problem is for the hitters who are also inexperienced and facing one of their peers for the first time. Last year, in coach pitch, it was the coach basically aiming at their bat so they could hit the ball. Now they are faced with the realization that the kid on the mound can't get the ball over the plate and is probably going to hit them with it. Only the kids with the best hitting mechanics and some training in how to avoid being hit when the ball is coming right at them will have the confidence to stand in there. Fear of being hit by the ball is a huge distraction and will affect the player's swing whether he has good mechanics or not.

Coaching Youth Baseball
Mastering the basics before attempting the advanced is true for every aspect of the game. It also holds true for coaches.

You probably would not be effective as a coach for a team of sixteen-year-olds with only one year of coaching which happened to be at the six-year-old level, on your resume. But if you continue coaching and increase your knowledge year after year, you never know where you may end up. Just like effort leads to change for a player, it also affects change for a coach. Many coaches make the bad mistake of thinking they know something when they first start coaching kids. Depending on your personality, you will either realize how little you know or you will continue thinking you know it all. If you realize how little you know, congratulations! You will have begun your journey to becoming an effective youth coach. If you think you know it all, you won't even be on the path and you will probably be affecting kids in a negative way. Unfortunately, in youth sports these days, it is common to see "know it all" parents and coaches and uncommon to see "learn it all" parents and coaches.

Play your role as a parent or coach by being a "learn it all" instead of a "know it all."

Mastering the basics as a coach means increasing your knowledge in many areas, not just baseball skills. When I first started coaching baseball, my son Phillip was seven-years-old. I continued to coach and, as each year passed, it became apparent to me that I had a lot to learn about the game and the challenge of making it fun for kids. I started reading about baseball, listening to other more experienced coaches, watching instructional videos, and watching Major League games as a student instead of just a fan. Learning the basics of technique and strategy will eventually lead to an awareness of what kids are facing when their parents are overbearing and expecting them to "just do it." It occurred to me early on in my career, however, that having knowledge about the techniques and strategies in the game of baseball was only part of the equation. In many ways, baseball is like the game of life; there are some basic moral principles to master before we decide to take on the title of "Coach."

Having humility, staying positive, controlling emotions, and showing leadership are more important than winning the game. Baseball happens to be a great way to teach these life skills. At the end of the season, if it's apparent that these character traits have not been taught to the young players, you have some work to do on your basic coaching technique.

Winning the baseball game is nice; being a winner in your personal life is nicer.

When your mind is open to learning, *you will learn.* When you lack humility, your mind will not be open to learning because your ego *will not allow it.* Your attitude as a coach will determine whether or not you will "master the basics before attempting the advanced."

Chapter 14

Learn All You Can, Teach, and Have Fun

A Parent's Role in Their Child's Skill Development: become informed so that you can instruct, and resist the urge to yell.

Who likes getting yelled at? I'm not fond of it, and I don't know anyone who is. If you find yourself yelling at kids on a baseball field, it might mean you have something more to learn about coaching kids in a game that is supposed to be fun. Too many times, kids are expected to perform skills they are not prepared for, and when they can't do it, they get yelled at. When adults' emotions get the best of them and yelling at kids is the result, it's not only the kids who are unprepared.

Becoming a student of the game and learning all you can about baseball is a good thing. It can help you gain proper perspective as a parent or youth coach by enabling you to understand what correct training is. But what many parents and youth coaches are missing is this: *It takes more than correct training to develop sustainable skills; it takes time.* If you don't understand and accept this, you will become impatient and overbearing. Just as big of a problem are the coaches who understand this truth very well, but instead of *taking the time* to teach, make sure the more naturally gifted players get the best opportunities while the rest become backup players as early as five and six-years-old. This usually results in more wins, but is ultimately a huge loss for youth baseball as the need for instant gratification erodes the process of teaching sustainable life skills the game offers for *all* kids.

As each year passes, it's becoming more common to see anxious adults expecting kids to perform skills just because they tell them to. Higher levels of competition and coaches' and parents' awareness of correct training in youth sports are becoming more unbalanced. Unfortunately, awareness of correct training is at the lower end of the scale while competition levels are skyrocketing. This dynamic hurts all players' progress, no matter what their level of talent, if they end up on a team that has uninformed, outcome oriented coaches and parents. These coaches and parents will be very focused on winning, but will be absolutely unprepared to win the right way. To help a child or team succeed in baseball, and ultimately in life, takes a disciplined person with patience and knowledge. You need an effort over outcome approach to coaching and the ability to be able to resist the desire for instant success which lives in all of us. It's rewarding, however, if you can do it whether or not you get to win the nine-year-old World Series and put a trophy on your mantle to collect dust, your trophies will be the kids you have affected in a positive way by teaching them at an early age how to get the most out of their ability. They will never forget it!

Your child's personal effort, not their accomplishments, is what will shape who they are on and off the field. Accomplishments fade with time, while consistent effort brings about more success. If your child gets passed over by some travel team or a middle school coach, help them understand that a good attitude and work ethic make good baseball players, not other people's opinions. By having the discipline to train properly and consistently, you take charge of your own destiny, and other people's negative actions toward you become less important. When your child doesn't make the all-star team, don't make it about the coach, umpires, or other parents who play politics to get their way. If you do, you will be off the path and your child's progress will suffer.

Play your role as a parent by teaching your child that a negative situation is temporary, but a person's positive effort can be permanent.

If your child gets a positive coach who is knowledgeable about what it takes to teach and coach young players, consider yourself lucky. Have respect and don't criticize them when something doesn't go quite like you imagined it would. If your child gets a coach that is not knowledgeable about baseball, but has volunteered their time because no one else would, have respect and support them as well. Your support might inspire them to learn more and eventually he or she may become a very effective youth coach. And by taking a positive approach, you may be inspired to learn more yourself.

Yelling at kids is not a legitimate coaching technique. It's a negative reaction displayed by coaches who are frustrated either because kids are not living up to their unrealistic expectations, or they do not understand the game themselves. There's a lot to know when it comes to baseball, and taking on the job as a volunteer coach or a paid coach, you have a responsibility to teach the correct rules, mechanics, strategies, and *attitude* for playing the game at the level you are coaching. Many parents and coaches go year after year without taking the time to increase their own knowledge, basically showing up unprepared. You wouldn't show up at your job unprepared. Why would you show up at the ball field unprepared, with the awesome responsibility of teaching baseball skills and, more importantly, life skills to young kids? If you can't find the time to educate yourself, you will focus on outcomes only and become impatient with kids. Do everyone a favor and let someone coach who continues to train themselves, and as a result, becomes more aware of a young baseball player's needs.

Over the past twenty years, America's favorite pastime has become more like a job for many kids. Parents' expectations are often geared toward college scholarships and professional careers instead of just having fun. With expectations like these, people lose patience and put too much pressure on kids, expecting them to do more than they are currently capable of. There is a sense of urgency that parents feel, and kids want no part of. One of the best simple examples is this: A young player, maybe eight or nine-years-old, is at the plate trying to get a hit. They swing the bat and their head turns with the swing, and they lose track of the ball. Everyone yells out the same correct information, whether they know what it means or not. "Keep your eye on the ball!" "Get your head down!" The problem is that this player may not have been trained to get their head down while they swing, so they can't do it during the game just because we want them to. No one took the time to teach it to them. Or, if it was taught, the concept of repeating something until it becomes automatic was overlooked. When this happens to a young player, I can only assume their coach or parent does not know the technique or understand the concept, so they can't teach it.

Having balance and seeing the ball all the way in can be taught to every player if a coach understands the importance and will take the time to teach it. It's not rocket science, but it does require patience. If you can't see it, you can't hit it. Most young players are essentially blindfolded because this most important aspect of hitting is not thoroughly taught before moving on to more difficult skills. When a player can't hit the ball, it's not much fun. Many times, when young players walk away from the plate in tears, it's because they have no idea why they missed the ball. They just know that they disappointed all the adults, adults who do not understand the most basic principle of training: *effort affects change.* These days, competition rules so expectations are high, which is all the more reason why kids need proper instruction in this crucial area of hitting before frustration gets the better of them. If you are not succeeding at a task, but keep doing the same wrong thing over and over trying to accomplish it and expecting a different result, you need to be enlightened.

By repeating poor technique, you will get better at poor technique. By repeating correct technique, you will get better at correct technique.

This principle is true not only for kids, but for coaches and parents as well, as it also applies to a person's attitude. If basics are not understood and taught by parents and coaches, young players who are struggling will eventually give up and walk away from the game all together.

On July 7, 2012 in Columbus, Georgia, two fathers got into a fistfight right before the medals were to be handed out for runner-up and champion of the District 8 Little League All-Star Tournament. Watching the video of the incident was unsettling, as a fun day at the ballpark turned into chaos. Everyone was affected. The two men were arrested, along with the wife of one of the men. The police report said that one of the men was playing loud music near the right field fence after his son's team had won the game. A mother from the other team came over and demanded that the music be turned down. The president of the league said "From my understanding, that is what caused it all. While that may be true from a police point of view, I believe there are other factors to consider. The two fathers in this case are like dynamite; society has become the fuse; competition the igniter. It's all connected."

When problems arise between parents and coaches at youth baseball parks, competition is usually the instigator. Lack of education is the enabler. If the emotions of competition outweigh perspective, there will be problems. This dynamic comes to play in a couple of different ways. When kids are very young (five and six-years-old), the goal should be a fun day at the baseball diamond, not drilling kids with technique that will bore them within five minutes. Instead, we are now seeing select travel teams at six-years-old where the emphasis is on winning. When that happens, inexperienced coaches are at risk of using these little six-year-olds to fulfill their own egos. Often, the coaches and parents are as much beginners as are the kids. Arguing with umpires, getting thrown out of games, and showing willingness to engage in heated conversation with the opposing team's parents are the unfortunate results of lack of experience and perspective. Coaches and parents who take the time to educate themselves put this kind of negative behavior behind them, gain perspective, and focus on the more positive approach of teaching sustainable skills. Not many people will actually get in a physical confrontation at their child's game but remember, disrespecting officials, coaches, the other team's players and your own need for instant results makes you a part of that fuse which is connected to dynamite like the two fathers mentioned earlier.

When kids are young, it's more important to be on a team that has a coach who is knowledgeable about, and able to teach, proper baseball basics than to be on a team with a coach who knows how to manipulate the other team's inexperienced young players by using trick plays or base-running tactics that have nothing to do with good baseball strategy. These plays will eventually be worthless and the players who have been taught real baseball skills will be better served. Remember that, for many coaches, winning is so important they will resort to anything to accomplish it. When coaching young players, we should consider whether the strategy we are using to win is appropriate or if it is just taking advantage of little kids who are inexperienced. Are we teaching kids how to play the game in a way that will benefit them later in their baseball life, or are we using strategies that will only work when trying to beat a six-year-old team, an eight-year-old team, a ten-year-old team? In the big leagues, there are unwritten rules of etiquette that are relative to the professional level of play and most managers and players take them seriously. One of the most common is: Don't steal a base with a big lead late in the game. Although this rule is usually adhered to in youth baseball, many others are not, such as: Don't take advantage of inexperienced little kids just because you can.

When this happens, it's an example of an adult who has not taken the time to learn much about their role as a youth coach and is willing to exploit the kids on the other team while they still can, just so they can win today's game. The coach is sending the message that winning is the most important thing. The unfortunate result of this kind of coaching is that players are being taught to win any way they can, even if it means using questionable and unsportsmanlike tactics. Because of this poor example, some kids will grow up and continue this disturbing tradition.

When the focus is on teaching and having fun, competition becomes a *tool* used by creative parents and coaches to instill the proper elements of a successful and happy life while developing the character traits needed to compete at a high level later in their baseball journey. Respect, humility, work ethic, good sportsmanship, positive attitude, and being accountable for your actions are the hallmarks of being a top competitor. When a coach's highest priority is winning games with a team of six-year-olds, these things will be hard to find because many coaches are willing to win at any cost. Using trick plays and only the so-called "best nine players" (which always include the coach's son, whether he is talented or not) is the norm.

As players grow older, the perspective about competition changes. If you are sixteen and were never taught the correct way to play the game or have not taken the time to develop your skills over the years, you can't expect to compete with those who have that experience. For those who *are* able to compete at this higher level, it will be necessary to continue the learning process in order to advance to the next level. If a player lacks humility and thinks he knows it all, he has peaked and other things will distract him from becoming the best ballplayer that he can be. He will no longer be focused on developing skills and the competition will prove to be too much.

Coaches at every age level should understand the responsibility that comes with the position, whether they are being paid or not. There are many skills to develop to be able to play the game and if a coach does not understand this and have a good base of knowledge himself, it sets the stage for many problems. Some players may be receiving lessons from a private hitting instructor. If you don't understand the basic hitting mechanics yourself, but insist that everyone do it your way because your ego gets in the way, there will be conflict.

As a parent, it can be frustrating to watch your child struggle to hit the ball, fail to make an accurate throw, or miss a ball thrown right at them. How you respond to this frustration is what will either help or hinder your child's progress. Raising your voice and giving vague advice such as "C'mon, make a good throw!" or "You gotta have that one!" is not instructive and only adds more pressure, making the task even harder for a kid who is just learning the skills. If you are one of these parents, you are not playing your role well and are focusing too much on the outcome. Many people have a natural tendency to focus only on the outcome and not the effort because of their own lack of knowledge. If you are doing this and refuse to change, get ready for a lifetime of frustration.

Awareness Is Where Learning Begins
Taking the time to read a book or watch a video on baseball fundamentals can really open your eyes to what it takes to play baseball successfully. You will become aware of whether or not your child is on the right track and you will learn some techniques that can help them. Once you have an understanding of your own child's abilities and interest level, you can begin a realistic approach to his or her training. If you remain unaware, it's not only your child's baseball journey you are going to affect in a negative way, but their whole life.

A parent's perspective and expectations have a lot to do with their child's experience as a baseball player: Will it be negative or positive?

When a kid is first learning how to hit the ball, for example, what is a good outcome? If you think hitting the ball is the only good outcome, you will be very disappointed and your child will pick up on this negative behavior. Most beginners will be turning their head and losing their balance as they swing. If they are doing this, you can't expect hitting the ball consistently as an outcome; it won't happen. First they must learn to achieve balance and keep the head still so they can actually *see the ball* as it approaches the hitting zone. When they can do this, you have a good outcome whether they hit the ball or not. This good outcome will lead to making contact with the ball because now they will see the ball better. You have to see it to hit it. Put a blindfold on a professional baseball player who has become a master of basic hitting mechanics and see if he can hit a 90 mph fastball. I doubt it.

As a teacher of baseball skills, it's frustrating for me to watch parents who struggle with their need for instant gratification. Frustrating because I know how it affects kids in a negative way. By becoming more informed about what it takes to develop sustainable skills or trusting and having respect for a coach who has taken the time to do this, you will gain new perspective about your child's baseball journey. This doesn't mean that baseball has to be your passion. Realizing that your kids are your passion should motivate you to learn all you can about something that until now you had little interest in. It's worth pursuing because you may find out things about yourself you never knew existed. Who knows, through your child's interest in the game, you may find out you like it more than you knew. If baseball *is* your passion, be careful not to become overbearing. Remember, a kid's passion is having fun and their level of interest may or may not be equal to your level of interest or expectations.

Most parents understand that the more they know about what their kids are interested in, the better prepared they will be to help them on their way. What makes it more difficult in sports is the competition and our perspective about it. The more knowledge you have about what it takes to develop skill, the better perspective you will have when it comes to competition. You will have respect for the difficult task your child faces. There are lots of books, videos, and helpful people around that can help you learn the correct mechanics of the swing and all other parts of the game. Yet, every year when baseball season starts up, you see well-meaning parents and coaches yelling out the wrong instructions. I say yelling out, because that is what people who know very little tend to do. Yell!

I remember early on in my coaching career realizing how much I had to learn as each year passed and my team's age group was older and more experienced. It can get to a point where you sense that the players themselves know as much or more than you do. It was at this point where I thought, "Either I have to increase my knowledge or step aside as a coach." I had always liked baseball, but it was through my son's love for the game that my passion grew. So, I decided to learn more.

Now, with this new level of commitment, my mind was open to new things and I gained an awareness of assets that were right in front of me. I noticed there was a parent on my team, Greg Gunnells, whom I knew and respected as a good person and who had a real baseball mind. He knew the game well, had played in college, and had previously coached. But his biggest asset was his knowledge about what it takes to play baseball at a very advanced level and his perspective about coaching the young kids on our team. He knew that having fun could not be sacrificed for the unlikely chance that these boys would become big leaguers. For some reason he was no longer coaching, so I talked him into being my assistant. He knew more than me, but he insisted that I be the head coach. I admired how comfortable he was on the ball field; like he belonged there. I wanted that! I learned more from him that season by just paying attention when he spoke and by watching him, than I had in all my previous seasons. It made me thirsty for more knowledge and I have never stopped trying to learn more.

Play your role as a parent by putting your ego aside, and for the benefit of the kids, learn as much as you can from others who know more than you do.

One of the greatest lessons I have learned is "if you can't demonstrate or at least explain it, you can't teach it." This was taught to me by my karate instructor, Bob Ozman, many years ago. Many parents and coaches resort to yelling out of frustration when things are not going well, instead of giving the players some specific information that might actually help them. When working with kids, all yelling does is take the fun out of it. Most coaches at the recreational level are volunteers. I applaud their efforts and can say with certainty that if they learn all they can, teach, and have fun, it will be one of the most rewarding experiences in their life that will bring joy to themselves and sustainable life lessons to the players they coach.

An additional problem for many volunteer coaches is coaching their own child. I did it for several years and found that it requires a unique set of skills to do it effectively. You are a parent and you have those same emotions that other parents have when it comes to their kids. Treating your son or daughter like just one of the players can be difficult. You may find yourself being too careful not to show favoritism to your own child and you may be too hard on them. Or you may have a tendency to think of the team as a workshop for your future major-leaguer. Neither of these approaches is fair to your child or the team.

When considering your role as the coach of your own child, it's beneficial to look at the big picture and resist the urge to make sure that they get every possible opportunity right now, to the detriment of others. If you are experiencing difficulty coaching or teaching your own child, there is nothing wrong with having someone else help. You just have to be willing to accept it. If you are fortunate enough to have a knowledgeable and caring assistant coach, you can ask him or her for help. There are also many very good professional instructors these days and it will be well worth it if your child shows an interest in getting the most out of their ability. Your own ego aside, what's important here is that your kid learns somehow, not that you have to be the only one to teach them.

If your child has a passion for the game, play your role as a parent by helping them keep that passion alive, not by making sure they are the shortstop in every game.

If your child happens to be one of the best players on the team, there is a great opportunity to teach them that with the gift of great talent comes the responsibility to help and encourage others (their teammates) who love to play, but are less fortunate when it comes to ability. This approach teaches leadership at a young age. If you can teach your child to have humility and to understand that they are on a journey to be taken one step at a time while learning baseball skills and life skills, their natural ability will reach its full potential and many opportunities will present themselves as time passes.

There is nothing more fun in baseball than learning and being able to compete. Without proper training, however, it's eventually impossible to compete at a high level. What I have noticed during my years of coaching is that by age thirteen and sometimes even earlier, the players who have not been taught correct skills have dropped out and gone on to other activities. The ones who remain have become proficient, and some of them outstanding. They have taken their natural level of talent and desire and trained to get the most out of their ability. And most likely, they had a realistic training regimen for their age.

This is much like a martial artist who trains for several years to attain the degree of black belt. If properly trained, they will have developed confidence to handle tense situations and be able to defend themselves if necessary. Students who have received a black belt from a school that awards them without putting in the needed time to really earn it may be in for a real surprise one day if faced with a real self-defense situation. The muscle memory won't be there and the correct reaction probably won't be either. Weak training leads to weak outcomes. The same thing can be said about a baseball player. If you have not put in the proper amount of time required to develop muscle memory to the point of being automatic during competition, you will have zero success against good pitching. Coaching is no different. It may not be physical, but if you have not prepared your mind with the proper knowledge and perspective to coach your current team's age level or ability, you will not find success. If ego is a problem for you, your response to lack of success will be to make excuses or blame others.

Baseball should be taught correctly at an early age and not be turned into some other game where coaches can affect an outcome by doing things that have little to do with real baseball, as it will be played later when the kids get older and more experienced. The sooner kids learn to play correctly, the more respect they will develop for the game and the better they will get at it. Teaching and making it fun is a coach's responsibility, not making sure the team wins no matter what the cost.

Coaches who take it upon themselves to learn more about the game will be more likely to steer clear of strategies that take advantage of the other team's young, inexperienced players, players who are still trying to overcome their own fears and nervousness. Instead, with proper knowledge, they will be trying to win the game with real baseball strategy and technique as it applies to the particular age group they are coaching. If you keep coaching, as I did, and find yourself in competitive travel leagues or coaching at a high school level or above, you will learn to take advantage of the other team's missteps, because by now they are very developed players who are expected to play at a high level and must learn to be consistent.

Those players who keep training to get the most out of their ability will find some success. Others will find that their interest in baseball no longer matches the required level of time and effort needed to stay competitive and will move on to other interests. There is nothing wrong with that. What is important is this: That the coaches they had during their playing years instilled in them the desire to do their best at whatever they decide to do and to learn all they can, teach, and have fun.

Chapter 15

Umpires

A Parent's Role in Showing Respect for Umpires: control your emotions and teach kids that it is their own preparation and efforts that can help win games, and that blaming umpires is only an excuse and a distraction.

Without umpires, there is no ball game. Yet, they are usually the first ones to get blamed when things aren't going our way.

Umpires will make mistakes because just like you and me, they're not perfect; they are human. Occasionally, an umpire *will* make a bad call, but it's more accurate to say that parents' and coaches' negative reactions are usually directed toward "close" calls and misinterpretation/ignorance of the rules.

Long-time umpire Mike Ladd puts it this way: "These aren't necessarily 'bad' calls, just calls that a coach or parent might not agree with. Coaches/fans need to remember that most umpires, if positioned properly, are typically much closer to the play and may have seen something not visible from the dugout or stands."

Mike is exactly right! When coaches and fans let their emotions overrule the truth—the truth being that the umpire is in charge and we should show respect—they are not showing their young players how to deal with the realities of life: that things don't always go your way, and when they don't, it's how you deal with it that reveals your true character. You can almost count on the fact that some close calls will not go your way. You can also count on the fact that some close calls *will* go your way because the other team faces the same dilemma. The interesting thing is that you never hear anyone say "boy, they really got ripped off on that one," when the "close" call goes your way and it obviously was a mistake by the umpire and should have been in favor of the opposition. We just ignore it and move on. We should do the same thing when *we* get a bad call. Just move on, and stay focused.

I've heard people say, "They've got an extra player on their team; how can we compete?" They're speaking of the umpire, of course, because things aren't going their way. People who say things like this are really just competing against themselves. The umpire has nothing to do with it. He is one of those elements over which you have no control. When a call doesn't go your way, it's important for the coach to stay focused so the players will remain focused. If you're a coach, change your response from one that lashes out at umpires to one that strengthens your own resolve to overcome obstacles. Placing too much importance on the umpire's role in our success or lack of success is a distraction we can't afford when trying to win a game. It takes the focus off of our own efforts. We need to be good enough as a team to absorb some bad/close calls by the umpire and still win. If the umpire has to be perfect in order for us to win, we have not accomplished much.

Play your role as a parent by teaching your child that they have control over their own efforts and attitude, and reflect it in your own behavior.

In the big leagues, when there's a close call, often the manager will storm out onto the field to argue. This can be very entertaining; some of them put on quite a show. The fans love it!

When it comes to youth baseball, however, no one has come to watch the coach. It's not entertaining when youth coaches argue with umpires. In fact, it can get pretty ugly. When parents, coaches, and fans disrespect the officials, the kids are watching and learning that when things don't go our way, we blame someone else. It's pretty easy to forget the errors that the team made, the lack of hitting, or the lack of hustle that may have made the difference in the game in spite of the close calls that didn't go our way.

Play your role as a parent by teaching kids that keeping your focus and putting the umpire's judgment call behind you will help you overcome obstacles and succeed.

If you are a coach and you want clarification about something, address the umpire in a respectful and professional manner. They're not going to overturn their call just because you want them to, but the real goal may be to influence the next close call. If you rant and rave and show up the umpire in front of everybody, what incentive have you given him to react in your favor next time? And there *will* be a next time. Also, keep in mind there are younger umpires in training. Nothing is more pathetic than watching an adult coach or parent try to intimidate a fourteen-year-old umpire. How can you go home feeling good about that? When this happens, perspective is lost. Don't let competition cloud the important fact that these are all young people and our higher goal should be the welfare of all the players and umpires on the field, not just our own kids.

Play your role as a parent by teaching your kids that the more prepared you are for excellence, the less likely it will be that you blame others for your failures.

By setting an example of personal effort and preparation, a parent or coach can teach kids that winning or losing has nothing to do with the umpire; he is a fact of life. It has more to do with ourselves and how we perceive the umpire: did the umpire make us fail, or did we make ourselves fail by losing our focus and placing blame on something over which we have no control? Teaching kids to overcome obstacles is one of the great values of youth sports. Let's make sure we don't miss the opportunity to instill this important life lesson every chance we get.

In the major leagues, when there are questionable calls by umpires, the interesting thing is that you never hear players or managers dwelling on the fact that the umpires missed calls during the game. They're not blaming them for the loss. Losing can easily be traced back to any number of things such as ineffective pitching, too many errors on defense, lack of hitting, or base-running mistakes, or maybe the other team was just better today. The reason most big-leaguers can put the umpire's calls behind them quickly is because they have learned they can't afford to let any negative thoughts linger in their mind. Sure, some players react negatively at first, but let it go fast because they know the game moves quickly and they have a job to do. They are well aware of their own level of ability and preparation and they reflect it in their behavior; they know how to win.

A winner realizes that personal effort is what can help them be successful, not arguing with umpires.

Many times in youth baseball games when we see people blaming umpires for causing them to lose, we can trace it back to any number of reasons such as those mentioned above in the major-league example. The difference is that many youth coaches and parents of youth baseball players can't put it behind them because winning is more important to them than player development, although they would never admit it. When winning becomes too important and a coach or parent starts blaming others for their team's or their child's lack of success, they're not looking at the whole picture, but just the part that serves them right now. In other words, they think, "I don't like what just happened concerning my child and there must be someone to blame." This attitude is just an attempt to feel good right now. The only problem is that when the ranting and raving is over, you're right back to where you started: *Your child probably just needs more practice and time to develop their skills.* This is where people have a choice: Either keep making excuses by blaming umpires, or start increasing your own effort as a player to become a better fielder, a better two-strike hitter, a better pitcher or catcher, a better base-runner and so on, and realize that it takes time to develop these skills and the responsibility is yours.

Coaches and parents should become more knowledgeable about the rules of the game and how to properly train their young ballplayers. By doing this you will be putting the responsibility for your outcomes where it belongs: *on yourself instead of on the umpire.* The umpire is just there to call what he sees. There are many resources available, such as training DVDs and books about baseball. If you're not using them because you think you know it all or you're not interested, you will not be very effective as a parent or coach. The more prepared you are as a team, player, coach, or parent, the less of an issue the umpire will be for you.

When parents are too concerned about immediate success, they will blame anyone, experienced or not, if their child is not getting what others are getting. They tend to make it about other people's efforts instead of their own child's efforts. Due to their lack of understanding on what it takes to become proficient at something that requires developing skill, they make it emotional. Being emotional is a wonderful thing if it's directed in the proper way. But when emotions are used to make an umpire, or a coach, for that matter, look bad, it contaminates the whole atmosphere. This can be contagious and if other parents join in this misguided effort, it can ruin the whole season for the team by taking the fun out of it for the kids. Have your perspective prepared for this because many times in youth baseball games there are lopsided scores, such as 19-1, 15-0, 28-4, and so on.

If you've been around youth baseball for a while, you have seen this. If you are new to youth baseball, you are going to see it before you know it. There are many reasons for these types of scores, but bad calls by umpires are probably not one of them. It's a fact of life that while kids are developing their skills and attitudes, there are going to be some games where your team is outmatched.

If you as a parent, coach, or player are not well prepared before the game, you will be more likely to blame others for your failure. *You will not have an understanding of what real preparation and effort can do for you.* How could you? You haven't done it. You have not experienced the benefits, which include increased confidence, knowledge, and perspective. I am talking about preparation and effort over a long period of time, year by year, as you grow on your baseball journey. Adults need to have their attitude prepared, and players need attitude and physical skills prepared—to be able to compete at their current level.

Many adults already have a good perspective because they got a strong dose of it growing up from their own parents, or maybe a knowledgeable coach. But when it comes to our kids, emotions play a big role and we should learn to control them, or it's easy to lose perspective. We all want our kids to succeed. There's nothing wrong with that. But when your kids make errors, or watch Strike Three go by without swinging, what are we going to teach them? That it's the umpire's fault? Kids need to know that it's not the umpire's fault and it's not their fault either, if they did their best. Sometimes during games we can get in that immediate gratification mode and forget that baseball is not an easy thing at which to excel. It takes time. We are on a journey and should enjoy it every step of the way, embracing every success and failure as a character-building experience and a normal part of our lives. If we do this and stay in touch with our own good efforts and training, we as coaches, parents, and players, can raise our level of awareness to a much higher plane. It will become clear that yelling at and blaming umpires is only a distraction and an excuse for our own poor efforts or lack of preparation. It must also be remembered that kids will not play like big-leaguers and we should not expect them to. If we put pressure on them to play perfectly or show them we are willing to blame umpires because we can't bear to see them fail, we will not be teaching them anything about how to succeed at baseball, or at life.

During our first game of the season while coaching a travel team with thirteen-year-old players, I witnessed one of the *worst* and *best* displays of parent behavior I had seen during my coaching career. From the very first pitch of the game, parents from the opposing team were disputing the home plate umpire's calls of balls and strikes in a very disrespectful way. I had never seen that before. Usually, it takes a few innings before people decide the umpire is at fault for their lack of success. For these folks, however, it didn't take any particular circumstance to set them off. Their goal was to intimidate the umpire. And it worked. Bill, the home-plate umpire, finally gave these unruly fans an ultimatum: "One more time and you will be asked to leave!" Well, that didn't take long. Within minutes they were at it again. Bill failed to eject them from the game. He was intimidated, and by failing to live up to his threat of ejecting the disruptive parents, he gave them even more power and their level of disrespect peaked. After hearing physical threats from some of these parents, a bystander called 911. Twenty minutes into the game we had the sheriff's department on the field instead of thirteen-year-old baseball players. The parents and players on my team made the choice to not say a word through the whole ordeal and I couldn't have been more proud of them. The parents were able to see the lack of importance a baseball game really has and found within themselves a higher purpose: teaching their kids more valuable life lessons. After about twenty minutes, the game resumed and I have to admit, I can't remember who won.

This example points out what can happen when an umpire doesn't take control of the situation immediately. In Bill's defense, you don't expect this kind of confrontation immediately. Umpires are prepared for some criticism because, unfortunately, it has become part of the game. Blaming the officials is disrespectful, but most umpires understand the emotions that are involved when it comes to parents and their kids, so some of it can be tolerated. What an umpire shouldn't have to deal with is intimidation. It's unbelievable that the sheriff's department should have to be called to a youth baseball game. No one can dispute the fact that the parents involved were lacking perspective. Unfortunately, with increasing importance being placed on winning, competition has taken on a whole new meaning and people are willing to disrespect anything that threatens their ambitions. What everyone should realize is, when we disrespect the officials we change the dynamic of the purpose of youth sports: to teach young kids life lessons. By blaming the umpires we sabotage the whole concept of teaching life lessons. How can you disrespect an official one moment, and pretend to be teaching sportsmanship the next moment?

Kids are very perceptive and intuitive. By the time they reach the age when they can play organized youth sports, they know the difference between right and wrong. There are times when the umpire gets it wrong. It happens all the time, even in the big leagues. It has nothing to do with a character fault; they just missed it. But when a coach or parent gets it wrong by disrespecting the umpire, the official in the game, they have failed in their duty as a responsible adult. Remember, if there were no umpires, it would basically be a free-for-all and who knows what would happen between the adults at the game? When I was young, kids would get together for a pick-up game with no umpires and it went just fine; but usually no adults were present.

It's easy to explain to a kid why the umpire might miss a call. It's hard to explain to a kid why their parents and coaches act like children and disrespect the ump when a call doesn't go their way. Every good parent I know teaches their children to have respect. Unfortunately, when the competitive spirit gets in them, some of these parents are unable to show respect themselves. They only see things from their perspective and they just have to be right. This is very confusing to kids because it doesn't represent doing things the right way. Because they respect their parents, kids model their parents' behavior and try it out for themselves by disrespecting not only the umpires, but their coach and teammates. I have coached and taught baseball for twenty years and have been a martial arts practitioner and teacher for forty years. I have witnessed lack of respect in baseball and other youth sports too many times to remember. In traditional martial arts, lack of respect is rare because it isn't allowed. Showing respect is taught and is more important than the technique itself. I think it would be a good idea to adopt this philosophy in baseball and other traditional youth sports. A martial artist without respect is a danger to himself and others. As mentioned earlier, parents who lack respect for officials are a problem in youth sports and can also become dangerous during a game between thirteen-year-old boys in which the cops have to be called to restore order.

Give umpires the respect they deserve. If you think it's an easy job, try it out for yourself sometime. If you've never done it before, you will quickly realize how little you know, and how much you pretended to know when you were blaming umpires for your child's failures during the game. Remember, using umpires as an excuse for losing only proves you are a loser. Teach kids how to be winners by keeping the focus on their own efforts and to respect the umpire whose job it is to call what he sees whether it goes their way or not.

Chapter 16

Parents

A Parent's Role in Their Child's Journey: Bring two rarely remembered facts into consciousness. Effort affects change, and you have no control over others.

You think your son or daughter has been treated unfairly by a coach? It doesn't feel good, especially for you, the parent. Now, here comes your response. Is it going to be positive or negative?

In August of 2010, there was a story published in a local newspaper about a parent punching a football coach in the face. He didn't think that his kid was getting enough playing time, so he confronted the coach about it after practice. The coach's response was "Why don't we discuss it later?" The father's response was "Why don't I just punch you in the face right now?" He ended up in jail and I can only imagine how embarrassed his son was. This attitude is becoming more and more prevalent in youth sports, although most parents who take this negative approach do it with a verbal assault instead of getting physical. The verbal attacks are usually more damaging to a sports program than the physical, although I did encounter a physical attack against myself in 1996 that could have had deadly consequences. A father, much like the one who punched the football coach, tried to hit me in the head with a metal baseball bat. Twenty years of martial arts training came in handy for me and I was able to subdue him and no one (including the attacker) got hurt. After giving my eleven-year-old players some perspective about what just happened and explaining that I am Coach Chuck and not Chuck Norris, we went on to have a fun and productive season. The "problem dad" was gone and, unfortunately, so was his very nice son. If this would have been a coach without my unique set of skills in martial arts, we might have had a very different outcome and that parent might be doing some hard jail time.

That same season I was asked to coach a girl's softball team. It was the first time my daughter had played and her team was without a coach. No one volunteered, so I took on a second team. Most of the girls had played for many years, and were very talented and a lot of fun. The parents turned out to be the worst I have ever encountered, even though not one of them swung a bat at me. Their verbal abuse was worse and spoiled the fun for everyone because, unlike the dad who swung the bat, these parents were allowed to stick around and continue imposing their negative attitudes on everyone, including their own children. I was able to defend myself against the parent with the bat more easy than the parents with the mouths. Although none of them volunteered to coach, they had no lack of opinion as to how it should be done and spent most of their time in the stands speaking badly of the coaches instead of cheering on the girls. Many parents make it about themselves and *will do or say anything* in a misguided attempt to achieve instant results for their kids, thereby robbing them of the *journey* and the valuable experience it offers.

For many parents, a negative response is the most familiar and likely when the child doesn't get what the parent wants—

or needs. After experiencing rejection or what you think is unfair treatment, it may feel normal and even good to lash out at the coach, or speak badly of him behind his back. A little bit of that can be forgiven. It's emotional. It's a normal response when first learning how to deal with rejection, failure, or unfair treatment when it comes to our kids. But if we dwell on that, our child's progress will suffer and we have missed the point. There can be many variables to consider before making a knee-jerk decision on our response.

First of all, it can take years to excel at a sport. It's a process of repeating the *correct* motions over and over many times, thousands of times. Slowly but surely, they will inevitably become reactions. If you don't understand and believe this truth, you will only see things from your perspective and are very likely to blame others for your child's failures, poor behavior, or lack of effort. Why wouldn't you? In your mind, there has to be a reason. Lack of knowledge about proper training, combined with an instant-gratification attitude, will lead you down the wrong path every time. Many times parents disrespect and blame the very coach who has helped their child in many ways instead of logically thinking it through. Believe me: *It's much easier to blame a coach than to put out the required effort to become proficient at a skill.*

Stop trying to *make* everything perfect for your child and start showing them how to cope when things aren't perfect. That's life!

Play your role as a parent by showing your kids the proper response to rejection, failure, and unfair treatment.

Is it bad-mouthing the coach or is it *realizing* that focusing on the coach as a problem will only slow down your child's progress? The goal is to help your child improve, not to make the coach look bad. This is where you should put your own ill feelings about a coach aside so you can stay connected to your child's real needs. What will help your child improve is consistent, correct training over a period of time, not using the coach as an excuse. Your child has no control over so many things, including the coach's behavior or preferences, but they do have control over their own effort. To parents, a coach's decision may seem unreasonable if they are only thinking about what makes them feel good. If feel-good results are what you seek, you will not be able to tell whether or not the coach is treating your child fairly. For example: It would be *fair* that your child should sit on the bench if they displayed a poor attitude during the game. In turn, it would be fair that a player already on the bench who is being respectful with a good attitude should enter the game.

Play your role as a parent by supporting a good coach's decision to hold your child accountable for their poor behavior or lack of effort.

The definition of "fair" for many inexperienced parents is that their child gets every opportunity, whether they deserve it or not. They may feel entitled because that's the way that they were raised. They only want what makes them feel good and they will do and say things to try and make that happen at the expense of the coach's reputation and their child's progress in baseball, and ultimately in their life.

Feel-good results will not help your child on their baseball journey—or in their life. Sometimes, at my martial arts school, a parent will talk to me about their concern that their child is not progressing as fast as others: "Why is my child not testing with the others?" This is a question that I have answered many times over the years. Most parents will show respect for my forty years of martial arts training and accept my explanation that their child is not quite ready, but occasionally an irritable parent will come up with their own explanation that goes something like this: "Well, Bobby is the same age as Jackson and they started about the same time in their karate training. Bobby just doesn't understand why Jackson gets to test first."

Actually, Bobby understands it one hundred percent but the parents can't stand the fact that some other student is moving ahead of their child. It's true that Bobby and Jackson were the same age and started at approximately the same time and have a similar level of ability. What Bobby's parents failed to realize—because they were so concerned about a feel-good result—was that Jackson comes to class three times a week and has never missed a week in over three years. Bobby typically gets to class once or twice a week and has missed several weeks and months over the period of time the two of them have trained. *They each made a choice concerning their training.* In Bobby's case, there were other priorities. Jackson made martial arts training his priority. Naturally, Jackson has progressed faster. They both may eventually reach the same goal, just not at the same time. The sad thing is that Bobby's parents would have been satisfied if Bobby would have been awarded the more advanced belt, even though he didn't earn it. This story represents a very basic principle in developing skill. *Effort affects change.*

Play your role as a parent by reinforcing this truth about training for the benefit of your child's progress.

This concept is understood by some parents but ignored by others who want to skip the basics and get right to the winning.

The Bobby and Jackson story is being played out at baseball parks all the time. Unfortunately, in our instant-gratification society, it's more common to see Bobby's situation. What makes things more difficult in youth baseball is that while some volunteer coaches have experience, many do not. Nor do many young parents. This sets the scene for misunderstandings due to lack of knowledge. When it comes to team sports, many people are very intolerant of anything except what will benefit their own child. Without specific knowledge, people will do and say things based on absolutely nothing other than their own emotions and egos. While this attitude may have the effect of making the parent feel like they're accomplishing something, all it really does is cause a distraction for their child in their pursuit of becoming a good ballplayer.

Providing your child with the opportunity for a "winning way" in baseball or any sport, has nothing to do with playing politics with coaches or making excuses, but everything to do with consistent training, correct technique, and a good attitude.

Inexperienced coaches still deserve your respect and are doing their best with what they know. Most of them are very good people. Their inexperience will not ruin your child's baseball career. Hopefully they *are* trying to learn more about teaching baseball skills to kids and are using resources available to them instead of relying on what they don't know. Once again, if a player will focus on developing skill through his own individual effort, there is no coach that can hold him back from eventual success.

Most coaches will have something to offer that will be useful to your child's development as a baseball player and person. By being tolerant and patient you will become aware of a coach's unique set of skills that could benefit your child. You will allow the situation a chance to be the best it can be. If you think the coach is unfair or ineffective in teaching skills, badmouthing him will not help your child get better. Asking to be on another team probably won't help either. You are still looking for shortcuts by thinking another coach will give you what you want. If your present coach is abusive, that's another story. The real answer for your child is to focus on something they have some control over: *their own preparation and effort.* They can choose to increase it at any time through personal training. By doing this they will be preparing for success, and in their pursuit, they will be winning! They will naturally expect success instead of failure.

Play your role as a parent by teaching your child that effort leads to change the next time something doesn't go their way.

"Hidden Passion"

Now, how about the level of passion required to excel at baseball? Do you have more passion for baseball than your child does? If you do, you run the risk of using your child to fulfill your own needs or dreams. This could be a very big problem if your expectations are too high. It will require a high level of interest on your child's part to meet your expectations and be able to compete at a high level of play. If you have it and your child does not, things will be out of balance. It will be only a matter of time until the relationship suffers, and you are likely to start blaming others in an attempt to make up for your child's inadequate level of interest.

Parents tell me all the time that for some reason, their child will listen to me when working on skills, but will tune their parents out. (I suspect it has something to do with patience and expectations.) This dynamic between parent and child seems to be fairly normal behavior, and I remember experiencing it some with my own son when he was young. Since he loved baseball, the important thing to me was that he learned proper technique, not that I had to be the one to teach him every little thing. Consequently, he learned many things from many different people.

These days, as a teacher of baseball skills, I have a different objective in mind from that of most parents. I am interested in what is happening *right now*, learning from the past, and not being overly concerned with the future. Emotions do not get in the way for me, so I am able to clearly see the steps necessary to help a student with individual issues such as poor balance or short attention span. Many times a parent is too concerned with the ultimate goal and is likely to grow impatient and skip steps in their quest to get there quickly. They want to see their kids hit the ball right now and don't understand why they can't "just do it." Some parents will even lack the presence of mind to just sit quietly while I am teaching their child how to hit. Even though they are paying me to teach their child, they will continually interrupt, as if they can talk their child into hitting the ball. It's easy to understand why this happens, but this lack of patience only frustrates the kid because they feel pressure to master techniques they are not ready for.

Play your role as a parent by becoming aware of the necessary steps to help your child get to their ultimate goal, and have the patience to let your child take these steps.

When you overwhelm someone, especially a kid who is interested in having fun, they will tune you out. Your expectations are too high, and you are not meeting theirs. They're not having fun. Whoever came up with the phrase "practice isn't supposed to be fun" couldn't have been more wrong.

A child's top priority is having fun. If kids aren't having fun, very little skill development will happen and the overbearing parent will become more frustrated, piling on even more pressure. You see the pattern. Having fun at practice doesn't mean that we will allow horseplay. It just requires adults to be creative enough to make it fun for kids while developing skills. If you keep your own passion under control and remain patient with appropriate expectations, your child will have fun and their skills will develop because you are allowing them the *time* to do it.

If your kid doesn't have a high level of passion or skill for baseball, does it mean that they shouldn't play baseball? No, but it might mean their interest lies only in playing the game at a recreational level, wherein their goal of having fun is easier to achieve. Once again, put too much pressure on your child because you have a burning desire (hidden passion) for them to be great, and it probably will ruin it for them.

Everyone has a passion for something, but many are not aware of what it is. Sometimes it's hidden deep down in ourselves, because there's never an opportunity to explore it.

Maybe you're hoping your kid will be an athlete like you were at their age. You encourage them to play baseball, which is fine. They might like it; they might not. If your expectations are in balance with their interest level, everything should work out; they'll probably enjoy playing baseball. However, if their passion lies elsewhere, maybe in music, and you shove baseball down their throat by making them be involved beyond their interest level, they will come to hate the game and disappointment is not far off. Remember, they may want to do both, but with the emphasis on where their passion lies. Instead of following your dream of having your child be like you were, let them follow their dream of becoming who they are.

Play your role as a parent by letting your child play the game on their own terms.

Several years ago, when I was coaching a team of twelve-year-olds, I met a boy named Ethan who had a conflict between his own passion and his father's misguided expectations. There were enough kids for two teams, so the recreation league where I was coaching decided to have two divisions. The idea was to put kids on a team with others of their similar ability. I was chosen to coach the advanced team. We held tryouts to assess their skills. Ethan wanted to play first base, so we let him try out there. It didn't go very well. He knew nothing about how to play the position. My biggest concern, though, was that he could not catch the ball very well, and I feared he would get hit in the face by a throw from a very developed player who threw really hard. By the age of twelve, some of the kids could throw the ball with a lot of velocity. This was a direct result of their natural ability and interest level, along with several years of working on their mechanics. They had trained properly. Ethan did not have a high level of athletic ability and obviously had not been training at all. His interest level in baseball was not in balance with his dad's unrealistic expectations.

Ethan did not make the advanced team. His dad was very upset and attempted to make it about me by spreading rumors that I was unfair and played favorites. He did what he could to influence other parents to share his opinion. He was somewhat successful and I got a call from the commissioner of the league. He explained to me that I would have to come to a meeting with the board of directors and the concerned parties to answer questions. I said, "No problem, I will be there." I anticipated a good outcome due to the fact that I had been coaching in the league for six years already with no problems.

It's interesting to note that the first time there was a problem is when the decision was made to have two teams, one of them an advanced, more competitive team.

The meeting was short. Ethan's dad was allowed to speak his mind and finally asked me this question: "What do you tell a twelve-year-old kid who doesn't make your team?" My reply was *"practice."* The very fact that he asked me a question like that, tells me that his own ego would not allow him to see what experienced coaches could see: that his son was not prepared to play at the more competitive level. If we had added Ethan to the team, we would have been setting him up for failure. We also would have been setting ourselves up for more confrontation from a father with unrealistic expectations. The meeting was basically over. The board of directors knew me well and knew that I treated people fairly. Fair in this case was that Ethan should play on the less competitive team. Of course, Ethan's dad refused to ever talk to me and influenced a few other parents that he knew to say nasty things to me or my coaches whenever they passed by. Instead of focusing on helping their kids get better, these parents decided that it was our fault that their kids did not make the more competitive team.

Your kids could end up wasting time doing what you want and never getting very good at what they want if you insist on excellence at something they have little interest in. Remember, they may have an interest in baseball, but only as a fun activity at an early age. Whether kids have natural ability or not, when it ceases to be a fun activity, the effort required and the will to do it will be out of balance. Travel/competitive leagues are now organized for teams as young as seven and eight-years-old and sometimes younger. Some of them have very skilled coaches with a good perspective. They can be a wonderful vehicle for the player with a burning passion, but they require a high level of commitment and are not for everyone. They are tempting because of the perception that these are the best players and you want your child to be one of them; but remember, just because it's called a travel team, does not mean the coaches are effective at teaching proper mechanics.

While some travel teams are excellent, others meet the description of "Daddy Ball," and you may be disappointed if your child is unfortunate enough to make one of these teams. You will realize later that the team's real goal is to showcase certain players whose fathers have a connection to the team. Your time and your child's time might be better spent working on honing skills with proper instruction over a period of time while playing at a local recreational league. I have seen coaches at the recreational level have just as much or more success teaching fundamentals as many travel team coaches who are obsessed with winning. A little research will go a long way before you decide where to play. As time passes, it will be your child's skill that counts, not what team they played on when they were ten-years-old.

By developing skills through proper training and many correct repetitions, your child will be creating opportunities for the future. Sometimes this is accomplished on a travel team; sometimes it's not. Effort affects change and your child's passion for what they are doing will determine how much effort they are willing to put out. The main thing is that they are having fun playing baseball. It is not a job.

The Journey: Staying on the Path
To say that baseball is not a job may seem like an obvious statement, but this is exactly what it becomes for a lot of kids who thought they were getting into something for the fun of it.

This is not the kind of journey that kids want to be on. Adults are the ones who turn baseball into a job by scheduling so many games that there is little time for any other activities during the summer. I don't know too many kids who would make this decision if it were up to them. When the season begins, kids are very excited to start playing games. If a parent says, "Guess what, Johnny? This year we are going to play eighty games," Johnny will be very excited at first because he doesn't realize that this means that there will be little or no time for any other activities. Dad forgot to mention that. The overbearing parent is usually serving himself by acting as manager for his "future major-leaguer." They are on their own journey that has very little to do with what is best for their child. When parents are overbearing, it more resembles a job for the kids because *results* are expected of these inexperienced players rather than effort only.

Adults understand that, at their workplace, results are expected *as they should be* and effort alone usually doesn't cut it. Many adults hold kids to this same standard, but it is not fair to do so.

Typically, adults have some level of expertise that got them the job in the first place. They have taken the journey one step at a time to get to where they are at this stage of their career. This is not the case when kids are starting out in baseball. They are always in over their heads due to the difficulty of the skills required to play the game, yet many parents and coaches expect too much too soon.

Veteran Los Angeles Dodgers sportscaster Vin Scully once commented: "This game is a constant struggle no matter how talented you are." Some parents are not willing to let kids take it one step at a time because they are so concerned about winning that their emotions often override common sense.

Play your role as a parent by remembering the steps you have taken on your journey and let your kids do the same.

One of the best examples of "being in over their heads" is nine and ten-year-old baseball. These are typically the first years of "kid pitch." At the first practice the coach will ask who wants to pitch. Everyone raises his hand. Most of the time, not one of them has been taught anything about how to pitch, yet parents and coaches are willing to put them out there and just expect them to somehow do it… on-the-job training, so to speak. The problem with this approach—which is repeated year after year at youth baseball parks—is that the kids end up walking one batter after another while the adults are yelling out all kinds of wacky pitching instructions. This is the best way to shatter a kid's confidence in himself, not only as a pitcher, but as a person. He has not been afforded the opportunity to learn a skill before he is expected to perform the skill. The fact of the matter is that he can't do it! The time for pitching instruction is long before the season starts, not at the first practice and during the games. Kids who receive proper instruction when they are eight-years-old are usually the best pitchers at nine because they can get the ball over the plate and they don't issue as many walks. The hitters are not very skilled yet so all that is required is some accuracy on the part of the pitcher.

Without proper instruction, the accuracy will not be there.

When we are overly concerned with results, we risk messing up the natural progression of proper training. By keeping the focus on effort (being present) instead of outcome (living in the future), a player can perfect their skills, and the day may come when those skills land them a spot on a select team such as a travel or high school team. Now, a certain level of play and concentration *is* expected if you want to be on the field instead of the bench. If you have done the work earlier in your life, your skills will be developed and you will have a chance of being a starter on the team, but there is still much to learn to be able to stay competitive with others of your similar or better ability.

The legendary coach, Vince Lombardi, said "The only place that success comes before work is in the dictionary ."

You cannot reach your goals without doing the work. You cannot stay on the path to success without taking each step. Being able to take all the necessary steps requires humility and patience as well. Without these two things, time will still pass but learning will not happen. As soon as you think your kid knows it all, they may also pick up on that way of thinking and start skipping steps. They will no longer be on the path and others who are will soon leave them behind.

Success between the ages of six and twelve, and success in high school are two very different dynamics. I have seen plenty of players have success when they were young because they were bigger and stronger than other kids, but never play in high school. Also, a player with natural ability may have a lot of success when they are young, but never play in high school.

There can be various reasons for this.

First, because they were bigger and stronger, they had early success, but since no one took the time to teach them the skills needed to play at a higher level, it was too late once they got there. They had developed too many bad habits.

Second, they may have been taught good technique, but had no interest in going through the necessary repetitions that ultimately teach the muscles and brain to react automatically.

Third, if a naturally talented player also has an overbearing parent, they may be burnt out on the game after spending every summer doing nothing but baseball. Now that they are a little older and more independent, they reject the game.

We had one such player on our nine and ten-year-olds' team years ago, when my son was nine. Mark was big and he threw hard. Whenever he pitched, it was an automatic win. The other team's players were very intimidated by him and afraid of being hit by the ball. He succeeded for a few more years, until the other players gained more skill and he did not. Mark never pitched one game in high school. No one had ever taught him the correct pitching motion. At ten-years-old, it seemed like he was successful, when, in fact, he was on a failed mission the whole time. His baseball journey was cut short due to lack of skill development. He had a very successful season as a ten-year-old. By the time he got to high school, no one cared and his love for the game was lost.

I have witnessed this scenario many times. With more awareness on the part of parents and coaches, some of these players who fell through the cracks may have found themselves still playing in high school or beyond if they had been taught correct mechanics when they were young instead of just relying on their premature growth spurt.

Keeping the Passion Alive
When my own son Phillip was playing between the ages of six and eighteen, it was a real learning experience for me as I wrestled with my own expectations and his. I could see that he had a gift for baseball since the age of four, when I would pitch him fifty balls a day and he would hit them with ease. We spent a lot of time over the years having fun playing catch, hitting balls, and fielding short hops. Phillip continued to improve with each year and had a very successful high school career. He had an opportunity to play in college, but chose not to play due to other interests and, at twenty-seven, began playing in an adult amateur league in California. Whenever my wife and I visit, we feel great joy in watching him pursue his boyhood passion; he still loves baseball!

I'm sure I made a lot of the mistakes that I talk about in this book, but I eventually realized what the real goal was: that my son was having fun and his love for the game of baseball would not be lost. We made a conscious effort not to burn him out on baseball. Every year we ended our season in July after playing about forty games. Our family then went on an annual fishing trip with my dad in Minnesota and Canada. I am positive that my son, would not trade that wonderful experience with his grandfather so he could've played another forty baseball games in the summer. Now, when Phillip calls me, it seems like baseball comes up a lot in our conversations. I am very thankful.

When your baseball season ends and your child is glad that it's over, take that as a clue. You may have played too many games or you may have reached just the right amount of games and now they are excited about their next adventure as a kid. Ending the season and wanting more is not a bad thing. It means the love for the game is alive.

Very few players will ever become major-league players or Division I college players. This is not the important thing. *Helping your child retain his love for the game is the important thing.* If he has the God-given ability, size, and desire, he may have a remote chance of becoming a professional. Having a dream of being a big-leaguer is not a bad thing. It's a dream that can help you reach your own full potential. We all may have envisioned our kids as a big-league player. It's a fun thought and is a part of the whole process. I have found that if a player possesses unusual amounts of ability it's obvious, and as each year passes if it remains obvious, who knows how far he can go? He will still need unusual amounts of passion, desire, and work ethic to go along with his great talent to succeed at the highest level.

I remember coaching a game at a local high school when the pitcher for the opposing team—a big lefty named Mike Minor—took the mound. Although none of us had ever met him, we all knew of him. Everyone in the area who followed baseball knew of him; he was rare. He was throwing the ball over 90 mph! The players on my team, very good high school ballplayers, were apprehensive about facing him at the plate. I remember telling them this: "Just try to make contact; foul one off. One day you may be able to say you played against a big-leaguer." Mike Minor made his Major League Baseball debut on August 9, 2010 for the Atlanta Braves. Unusual ability, perseverance, good attitude, desire, and passion got him there.

A wise friend of mine, Mary MacDonald, once told me that just because someone is good at something, *it doesn't mean that they want to do it*! This is good advice to remember, and it can be helpful as your child grows into who they really are. When it comes to baseball, many kids enjoy playing all the way through high school, but do not find in themselves the level of desire and commitment required to play on a college level. To excel at *whatever* level your child is playing at, desire will have a lot to do with it. Even if you have talent, without desire you will be of little use to your teammates or yourself. You will not put out the required effort to be consistent. At higher levels of play, as in high school and especially college, the commitment is substantial.

The real benchmark for whether a player continues to follow their initial interest in baseball, or anything for that matter, is whether or not they continue to enjoy it. If your child continues to enjoy baseball, there is a real possibility of some success sooner or later, simply because they won't quit. Will it come in the way of being a big-league player or a successful high school or college career? Who knows? Natural ability, desire, work ethic, persistence, and level of passion will all play their part. A little luck doesn't hurt either. If a player is taught the proper mechanics at a young age and puts forth a good effort, skill will continue to develop and opportunities will be created, much like a farmer plants seeds in the ground, cares for them and watches them grow, then harvests the crop later.

There is never a guarantee of success, even with a good effort. But one thing is for sure: without good effort, there is not much chance of success. You will be counting on being lucky. When success does happen, be thankful.

In today's youth baseball, there are a lot of highly competitive leagues. This has had the effect of putting pressure on athletes at a very young age.

A mother of one of my students once said to me, "Well, if my son doesn't make the middle-school team I guess it's time to hang it up." Wow, time to hang it up at twelve-years-old! I wasn't sure if *she* was giving up or her son was, but I asked her this question: Does your son love to play baseball? Her answer was an emphatic "*Yes!*" I knew he had enough talent and experience, so my advice to her was, if it's true that he has a love for it, all he has to do is continue on his path and not quit. Perseverance will sustain him. By not quitting he is affecting his own outcome and will be creating opportunities that otherwise would not have happened. By combining this positive approach with a healthy mind, body, and technique-training program, his opportunities are ahead of him. Many others, some of them very talented, who make the middle-school team, will quit for various reasons and never play in high school.

We don't always get the opportunities we want, when we want. But keep up the good effort and keep your passion alive. There are more opportunities waiting and by keeping a positive attitude towards yourself and others, eventually you will get yours. Conan O'Brien, former host of *The Tonight Show*, said this during his final show on January 22, 2010: "Nobody in life gets exactly what they thought they were going to get. But if you work really hard and you're kind, amazing things will happen." This is a very simple principle that applies not only to a famous entertainer, but also to a young baseball player.

Sometimes, when you finally get an opportunity, people say, "He got lucky." They were right. Lucky enough to be able to continue doing something you love and are good at. By your own good effort, you made sure of that. It is said that you can make your own luck. What that statement really means is that *by putting forth consistent good effort, opportunities will be created.* If you are lucky enough to get a good teacher or coach at a young age, consider that a privilege. Not everyone has that good fortune. Contrary to popular belief, you do not need to be the most talented to have success. You just need someone who cares enough to teach you that effort affects change, and that mind, body, and technique are equally important when it comes to developing skill. They are one.

Beyond High School

If you define success for your child as being a starter on a Division I college team or a major-league player, you may be disappointed. That may be *your* dream, but your child may or may not have the proper tools to pull it off. If a player has the ability to play on a Division I level in college or professionally, it's usually obvious by the time they graduate from high school, especially to experienced coaches and scouts. By allowing your child to follow an honest path of skill development over the years as they grow through their baseball experience, you will also be well aware of their true level of ability and interest. If you interfere by making excuses, blaming others, or playing politics with coaches, you may never learn the truth about your child's real abilities and end up sending them in the wrong direction. What would be better? Sitting on the bench on a Division I team or being a starter at a junior college? If you love to play baseball, I am going with being a starter at the junior college. Why not be playing instead of watching? You are there to get an education. That is where your future lies, not on the baseball field.

In his book, *A Zen Way of Baseball*, the great Japanese baseball legend Sadaharu Oh, who hit 868 homeruns as a professional player, says "For most boys who play high-school baseball, victory and defeat, at least in terms of baseball, are futureless." He had this realization after his high school team blew a big lead in a game that would either send his team to the championship game or end their season. They lost, the season ended, and, for most of his teammates, it was the end of their dream of a baseball career. But it had nothing to do with the loss of that game. For various reasons, there never was a future for them in baseball. The sting of this very disappointing loss soon subsided and they went on to other careers. But for Sadaharu Oh, it was the beginning of another phase of his baseball life. He was that rare exception.

Once again, through your good effort, you never know where you will end up. A future in baseball as a professional is unlikely, but good effort is always rewarded. Life can be full of surprises. Maybe your son or daughter has the talent to be a great coach. What a success! Not everyone has the ability to do that, although many are doing it anyway, sometimes to the detriment of certain players. Many coaches may have been good players themselves at one time, but do not have the skills or patience required to teach young players. There are different levels of skill and talent when it comes to teaching and coaching as well. Helping your kids follow their passion, develop their skills, and assess their natural gifts and talents as they continue on their journey is all you can do. The rest is up to them.

Ethan's Gift

Ethan's gifts, talents, and passion were not in baseball, but in music. My advice to Ethan's dad after Ethan didn't make my baseball team was that you must practice to develop your skills. Ethan practiced, all right, but it wasn't baseball. Three years after Ethan had tried out for and not made my baseball team, we met again. This time it was in the music room at his high school. Another passion of mine allowed me to reconnect with Ethan. Since I had previously made a living as a musician, my daughter Shelley had taken it upon herself to volunteer me for the position of jazz band instructor. The band director knew very little about running the jazz band, and she was more than happy to have a former professional musician help out.

We set a time for the first rehearsal. Many interested student musicians showed up. One of them was Ethan. He opened up his case, pulled out his guitar and started playing, and my jaw dropped! This was quite a different realization than when I had originally met him at first base back on the ball diamond when he was twelve. Ethan was now fifteen-years-old and obviously had talent. He had been practicing, and I soon realized he had a *passion* for music. I taught the jazz band for the next four years. We eventually recorded a CD at a professional recording studio. Ethan was a standout soloist on the CD. We also played at several jazz festivals in

the area and many school events over the years. Ethan gradu-
ated and got a music scholarship at a very good private college. He asked me to write a letter of recommendation when
he applied for the scholarship. I was honored to do it.

His dad still has not spoken to me.

Chapter 17

Stretching and Proper Breathing

A Parent's Role in Stretching and Proper Breathing: have the discipline to teach these essential preparation tools.

The benefits of learning to stretch at a young age are enormous. For a young player, learning to stretch has less to do with becoming flexible now, and more to do with *establishing a routine that will help them stay flexible for the rest of their life.* It requires discipline to learn the stretches correctly and do them on a consistent basis. It's a great way for a coach to teach discipline because, while stretching as a group, you have everyone's attention. You will have some players try to get away with doing the stretches the easy way by doing them incorrectly. For some, they have never felt their bodies in this way. They feel the burn of the stretch and instead of holding it, they will give in to it. But with encouragement and instruction, they will learn to overcome the tendency to give in and welcome the chance to better themselves through stretching. Not only will you become a looser player through stretching, but you will come to know your own body better. Also, some stretches, like standing on one leg and pulling your knee to your chest, are great for improving balance when done on a regular basis. A stretching routine also provides a good opportunity to get your mind on the activity that you are stretching for and let all other distractions go.

Play your role as a parent or coach by teaching preparation skills to young players so they can get the most out of their ability and increase their chances of having fun.

Kids want to play baseball because they think it's going to be fun. If preparation is not a high priority for parents and coaches but winning is, the kids' fun will be short-lived, and an opportunity to teach an important life lesson will be missed.

Before picking up a glove or a baseball at practice or a game, all players should jog around the field or do light calisthenics to achieve a light sweat. This will increase body temperature, and increase blood flow to the muscles. They are now ready to stretch. After the stretching routine is complete, it's time to get their gloves and warm up their arms. This is proper preparation. Teach it to kids at a young age and they will thank you for it when they are older.

It's never too early to teach kids how to prepare for a physical activity like baseball. If you don't teach it, they won't do it! In the martial arts classes that I teach, we *always* warm up and stretch before doing anything else. It wouldn't make sense not to. The kids have come to expect it. We are preparing our mind and our muscles for the class or competition. When you go to a youth baseball park, it's hard to find correct stretching going on anywhere. You are more likely to find horsing around while parents and coaches are trying their best to instill order. Finally, after wasting the time that would normally be used for warm-up and stretching, they get the kids together, give them a few empty threats about goofing around at the practice, and then the practice begins. They are off to a poor start! There is no reason why stretching should be part of martial arts, but not baseball. I think youth baseball associations should make it mandatory for coaches to teach this kind of preparation. The additional benefit it has for young kids is that you are teaching them self-discipline by being consistent with a routine. Skipping these steps and letting kids go right to practicing or playing the game shows a lack of preparation and the disappointing results of this kind of coaching will show up not only during the game, but in other areas of their life as well.

Most adults know a few stretches that they can show kids. If not, there is plenty of information readily available on the Internet, in books, or through people you know who have experience with stretching. If you notice a coach putting his team through a warm-up and stretching routine at the ballpark, take some time and watch what he is doing, and don't be afraid to ask questions.

Play your role as a parent or coach by learning correct stretching technique and have the discipline to be consistent and make it part of the routine before practice and games.

Remember, the goal when teaching young kids, who are already pretty limber, is not to teach them every stretch in the book, but to help them develop the good *habit* of stretching so they will make it a natural part of their competitive experience as they grow older.

Here are some basic guidelines for stretching when coaching young players:

- Learning to breathe correctly while stretching and throughout the activity is important. It supplies oxygen to the muscles and adds rhythm to your stretches.

- Breathe in before a stretch and breathe out as you move into the stretch with a controlled, fluid motion.

- Concentrate on the part of the body you are stretching and once you feel mild tension, you have reached your maximum stretch.

- Breathe freely and hold it for ten to fifteen seconds *without bouncing* while the muscle relaxes (static stretching).

Also include stretches that involve movement such as arm and trunk rotations, squats and lunges (dynamic stretching). These will give more functional flexibility to baseball-specific movements.

If you are a coach or a parent helping out, forget these words: "no pain, no gain." You should not feel pain when you stretch, but remember that many kids will have such a low tolerance to pain when they first start they will think that everything hurts. They may be reluctant to feel even mild tension. Help them understand the difference by knowing the difference yourself. Remind kids that stretching is not a competition with others, but a personal effort.

Here is an excerpt from the book *Ultimate Flexibility: A Complete Guide to Stretching for Martial Arts* by Sang H. Kim. Mr. Kim is a martial artist with an M.S. degree in sports science, and his book is one that parents and coaches should read and understand, and that kids will eventually understand if they are given the opportunity to practice proper stretching on a regular basis.

Improve Body Awareness

Mr. Kim states that "Through consistent, mindful stretching you develop and strengthen the connection between your mind and your muscles. Each stretch creates a unique sensation in a specific set of muscles that you use in your martial arts (baseball) practice. By paying careful attention to these sensations, you will develop a detailed knowledge of how your body works, which muscles are used for what type of movements, how your muscles and joints interact, and where your weak points are."

Proper Breathing

Focusing your mind on the task at hand and letting go of other distractions is the key to getting the most out of your ability and training. Taking a breath before every pitch and every swing helps keep your mind on an even keel and relaxes the muscles at the same time so that you can be loose and quick when necessary. You are not only preparing yourself for what you expect to happen, but what you do not expect.

The next time you watch a Major League Baseball game, watch the pitchers.

Pitchers will breathe in and exhale before every pitch. There is a reason they do it and it is the same reason a Little League player should develop the discipline to breathe before every pitch and every swing. It relaxes the muscles and focuses the mind. The very nature of competition can bring on tension if we allow it to happen. Often, a young player will purse their lips and tighten up before they throw a pitch or swing the bat. Breathing in through the nose and exhaling through the mouth can help keep players from getting tight. If they tighten up, they will start thinking and their reactions will be slow.

Yogi Berra said it best: "You can't think and hit at the same time."

Play your role as a parent during games by making sure that your language is positive and refrain from shouting out instructions that will only make your child start thinking and playing tight.

The time for analyzing and working things out is during practice. By being patient and encouraging during games, you can help your child play loose and on automatic. You can remind your child to stay loose by breathing instead of yelling out "throw strikes" or "get a hit," which will cause them to think instead of trusting their training and letting it happen. Cheering is great, but screaming vague instructions at a kid while he is trying to concentrate on seeing a small round ball coming at him from 45 feet away and trying to hit it with a round bat is no easy task, especially if he is afraid of getting hit by it. The best thing that I have ever seen a nine-year-old kid do in this situation during his time at bat was this. The crowd was yelling out all kinds of instructions to this young player. Coaches, parents, you name it. Everyone had advice for him on how to hit the ball and I was feeling sorry for the poor kid, who was just trying his best to get a hit. Finally, after a couple of pitches, he stepped out of the batter's box, turned to the crowd and in a disgusted tone of voice said, "I know what I'm doing!" I wanted to shake his hand. Out of all the people in the crowd, adults included, only a nine-year-old kid got it right! It was game time. He could only do what *he* knows.

Kids will play loose if they trust their parents to be understanding and encouraging when failure happens. They will feel free to take chances based on the amount of training they have received. By taking chances, they will be putting their training to the test. They will see what works and what doesn't. Breathing before every pitch, every swing, or anytime they feel pressure will become second nature because they will come to realize that staying loose is what will help them succeed, not trying so hard that they get tight and their reflexes get slow.

Kids are fast learners when the adults around them know how to play their role. This is the only way they can really improve. If parents and coaches make a habit of showing disappointment when kids fail, it will cause them to play tight and they will never see what those kids are capable of. They will only see what they are not capable of—playing loose.

Stretching to Prevent Injury

Playing baseball requires your body parts to work together. If any part is not functioning at one hundred percent, another part may overcompensate and, with enough force, an injury can happen. Here is an excerpt from the excellent book on training called *52-Week Baseball Training*, by Gene Coleman, who is a strength and conditioning coach for the Houston Astros. This information is geared more toward older players, but it is useful information for a parent to be aware of if your child retains his passion for baseball and hopes to progress into high school baseball and beyond.

In his book, Mr. Coleman writes:

What happens when your muscles are stiff and tight? If the tightness is in your leg muscles, your stride length will shorten and your ability to accelerate and run at top speed will be limited. If it occurs in your trunk, trunk rotation and throwing and hitting force will be restricted. If it's in your arm or shoulder, range of motion, speed, and accuracy will be reduced. Can tight muscles increase the risk of injury? Yes. Short muscles produce less force and fatigue more quickly than long muscles. Fatigue increases the risk of injury, especially when muscles have to contract with a lot of force to produce quick movements and bursts of speed. Tight muscles are also associated with an increased risk of stress fracture and knee injury. Muscles are the primary shock absorbers in the body. Every time your foot hits the ground, your leg and foot muscles absorb an impact of three to five times body weight. Because tight muscles can't absorb much force, the force is transmitted, to your bones.

Swinging a bat involves the whole body. After inhaling through the nose and exhaling through the mouth, you take a balanced stance with the knees flexed and the weight on the balls of your feet. Your body is loose and your hands and bat are in the launch position and moving slightly even before the ball is pitched in order to get your rhythm and relieve tension. As the ball is being delivered, the hands go back and the forward leg touches down lightly on the ball of the foot. The hips and lower back deliver the power from your legs to the upper body as they turn and bring the hands along with them in a direct path to the ball. Your eyes have been focused on the pitcher's release point, your head has remained still, and the forehead goes down during the swing to keep the eyes on the ball.

If you are able to accomplish all of this during the swing, you have a good chance for success. This is easier said than done. Not only must you understand the mechanics of the swing, but breathing and proper conditioning of the muscles are essential for total preparation. You are exerting a lot of force during the swing and if any of the body parts are out of sync or muscles are stiff, injuries can happen because one part is weak in its execution and another part overcompensates for it.

During my years of coaching I have seen players injured in various ways while swinging a bat. Young kids who are just learning will swing right out of their shoes while trying to hit the ball as hard as possible. As they are spinning around due to poor balance, an ankle gets twisted or they hit themselves with the bat as they are falling to the ground. Older kids and adults have a different problem. They may have developed better balance, but if they have not established good training habits over the years, chances are that they haven't been stretching properly and certain parts of their bodies will not be prepared for the intense force an older and more powerful body can deliver. The worst case I have witnessed involving a high school player was a player breaking his leg during a swing. Even if injuries like these are rare, one thing is certain: If you are not loose, your swing will suffer.

The first thing I teach a young ballplayer about hitting is that it's what he does before he swings that counts. The same thing is true for pitching, infield, outfield, base-running, and every part of the game. It is mentally and physically preparing yourself for success by stretching and proper breathing as you grow one step at a time on your baseball journey.

Chapter 18

The Volunteer Coach

Y ou've volunteered to be the coach for your son or daughter's team. All the parents thank you and couldn't be more
appreciative. They understand the huge commitment you have
made to take on what can seem like a full-time job. They realize the responsibility that comes with coaching and see you as
a real leader for taking on a role in which they can scarcely see
themselves. As you spend hours, days, and weeks formulating
a plan, you realize you will need some help, so you call on one
or two willing parents to assist with scheduling and being an
assistant coach.

It's time for the pre-season parent meeting where you out-
line your game plan and philosophy about coaching young
kids. You let the parents know that you're a very fair coach
and you have an "effort over outcome" attitude when it comes
to training young ballplayers. After explaining that giving a
good effort is the most important thing we can teach the kids,

and it's what will lead them to becoming better ballplayers and people, everyone is very pleased. After all, this is exactly what every good parent would teach their kids, whether it's baseball or taking out the trash. The meeting continues and everyone agrees on everything: "It's for the kids!" and "It's gotta be fun!" are the dominant themes. You say "See you on the ball field; let's have a fun season!" The meeting is over; everyone shakes your hand and thanks you again for taking the time to coach their kids. Things are going well and you are gaining confidence that you can really do this. Everyone is so supportive! Then, the first game starts.

One thing you will notice about parents who have kids in competitive sports is this: *If everyone gets their way every time, there is never a problem.*

The longer you are a coach, the more you realize that the parent/child dynamic will never change; it's emotional. Most, if not all, parents would like to think of their child as very talented. There is nothing wrong with that, because they may be very talented. Sometimes, though, they are very talented at things other than baseball. When it comes to competition, many parents make the mistake of comparing their child to others. Doing this clouds their mind of a clear vision of their own child's abilities and interests. With this in mind, the goal of the volunteer coach should be to recognize the level of ability in every player and help them get the most out of their ability, whether they are naturally gifted or not. Communicating their kid's role on the team to parents can help. The sport of baseball has many specific roles to fill in the makeup of a team. If your child is not a fast runner, for example, being the leadoff hitter is not practical. The goal of the parent should be to recognize and accept the level of talent and desire *their* child has, not to compare them to others, and to be ready to assist the coach in any way they can to help their child *have fun* and improve.

As a volunteer coach, you can help parents understand this concept by being the example. Even though their physical abilities are not equal, you can treat players equally (including your own child) as human beings. Parents will usually (not always) accept your assessment of their child's ability if you are treating all players fairly. *"Fair" doesn't mean that all players get equal playing time. Fair means that all players are treated equally based on factors over which they have control: their effort and attitude.*

Most people understand that, in order to be competitive, the players with a higher level of skill will be used more. That's not the issue. The issue is the balance between letting talented players remain in the game, even when displaying a bad attitude, ignoring less talented players who possess a good attitude, and teaching all the players that effort and attitude is number one. The best time to do this is at the very beginning of the season. Teach players, naturally gifted or not, that lack of effort or poor attitude will get them to the same place every time: the bench!

A person's ability or inability to show good effort and attitude (mental preparation) is what will determine their ultimate success in accessing their full physical capabilities.

Anyone, no matter what their level of skill, can choose to increase their own effort toward skill development at any time; no one can stop them. They can also choose to have a good attitude. I have found that once I follow through on my promise to bench players with poor attitude or lack of effort, they turn it around quickly and it benefits not only them, but the team as a whole. I have known many people who have changed their poor attitude, increased their effort, and by doing so, have improved themselves not only as baseball players, but as human beings. As a youth coach, don't make the mistake of letting players think that you value them based on their talent level only. If you do, you will send the wrong message to both the naturally talented and less naturally talented kids that somehow their skill level defines who they are.

As mentioned earlier, your definition of "fair" should include benching talented players who display a bad attitude. Many win-at-any-cost coaches fail in this area; they will never bench their so-called superstars. They've convinced themselves that being fair is just making sure that every player gets in the game, never mind if it's just the last minutes or even seconds of the game. Although this may make the coach feel good, it can be embarrassing to a young player to be an afterthought in a game that's basically over. To help avoid this situation, all players should get equal attention from the coach at practice. This is where a coach can find each player's individual strengths.

If you overlook players at practice, you are likely to overlook them in games.

Practice is where confidence is built, not only for players, but for coaches to gain confidence in players. By paying attention to all players at practice, you will no longer have the mindset that letting certain kids play will hurt your chances of winning. You will be confident as a coach that you can find a way to help each kid perform their role on the field, and not just on the bench. Also, when kids are young, playing the so-called *best nine* doesn't impress parents who just want their child to be treated fairly. Unfortunately, in our outcome-oriented society, this unfair approach to coaching young kids is very common. It's beneficial for a coach to consider the context to which they are coaching. Making sure that you are fulfilling the role which is expected of you is the important thing: Are you a major-league manager who is paid to win games? Or are you a volunteer coach whose responsibility it is to teach every kid the basics of the sport, and when the opportunity presents itself, the life lessons that are so often present?

Perform your role as a youth baseball coach, treating all players fairly by remaining aware of the context in which you are coaching. This will help you choose the appropriate response to a player's effort and attitude, good or bad.

Everyone is born with unique abilities. Some kids are natural musicians. Some are natural athletes. Who knows? But one thing is for sure: every team will have kids with different natural abilities sharing the same bench. Your job as a youth coach is not to weed out the weak baseball players, but to help all the kids become stronger by being strong yourself. Don't cave in to overbearing parents with strong personalities who impose their selfish desires on everyone at the expense of young children. During practice, be a leader and help all the kids reach their full potential, emotionally and physically. During games, get kids off the bench and on the field by showing every player you care about them, and mean it.

As a coach, you can recognize the athletic potential in all your young players by making it about the players, not yourself. It's a simple formula, but for some, it's very hard to follow. Coaches who make it about themselves are the ones whose motives are directed toward selfish outcomes, such as winning the game no matter what the cost. If you coach like this, perspective will be lost and you won't see the whole picture. You won't recognize the development of every player on your team, only the naturally talented ones. You will tend to ignore the less athletic players because you believe they can't help you win. Remember, youth sports are not meant to be entertainment for adults, but a nurturing process for kids.

Being a successful youth coach entails more than winning games. It means you're teaching kids how to have respect, self-discipline, self-confidence, and self-control, and to put forth good effort with a good attitude. Youth coaches who do not possess these qualities themselves will become win-at-any-cost coaches because that's all they know. Winning will become top priority for these coaches and the rest of the life lessons will be lost.

Coaches should make personal effort and attitude a priority when trying to win games. By doing this, players will learn this life lesson and soon realize what it takes to be on the field instead of the bench. Stick to your guns on this and every player will benefit because it's a fair approach. They will all feel that they have an opportunity to contribute and get the most out of their ability. You will now have a real sense about every player's ability, not only physically, *but their ability to show respect, have a good attitude, and put forth good effort.* Without these crucial attributes, a player's full physical potential will never be reached, because they will be competing with themselves.

Their own arrogance and laziness will ultimately win this battle. Teaching players this concept is teaching them how to win for the future, one achievement at a time.

Kids will respond to instruction in their own way and in their own time frame. A naturally gifted player will be able to successfully execute the basics in the first few attempts. A child with less natural ability might struggle with the simplest technique if they have never done it. This can be a problem for an inexperienced youth coach, especially an outcome-oriented coach whose measure of success is winning games; what should we do with those less-talented players who only help us lose? It's a challenge for a youth coach to meet the needs of all players, naturally talented or not, but it has to be a priority. *When they are young, every player deserves equal attention and caring from their coach.*

What players do with it is their choice, of course, but a coach of young players has to be patient and encouraging, realizing that they are the mature one, not the young player.

Don't be fooled, however, by the player with less natural ability. Many times—with encouragement from adults—a struggling player's level of desire is higher than that of the naturally gifted player, and because of their ability to work harder, they will surprise everyone except for the most enlightened coaches who have seen this before. Encouraging and caring coaches can help kids who are struggling with techniques that are unnatural for them by teaching them that frustration and disappointment can be turned into success if one does not give up. *When someone is not 100% committed, they will always find a way to quit. When someone is 100% committed, they will always find a way to continue.*

With a high level of desire and commitment, a player can persevere, be patient, and endure the ups and downs that come with training, especially training to achieve excellence. This applies to everyone, regardless of ability. Remember that a player might have a high level of ability in baseball, but not the required level of commitment or *humility* to compete at the next level. Because of this truth, many naturally talented players who succeed early on quit for various reasons when they get older. When they were young, these talented players were given every opportunity to be on the field instead of the bench because of the desire to win on the part of coaches and overbearing parents who influence coaches. Meanwhile, kids with less obvious talent but a high level of desire to improve their skills are overlooked because of the must-win attitude of many coaches.

It's important to give all players equal attention when they are young, not only because they deserve it, but also because you never know who has it in them to step up and take it to the next level. They all deserve a chance and a knowledgeable coach who cares can make sure that that happens.

Play your role as a youth coach by redefining "must-win" in this way: Every kid, regardless of natural ability, will receive equal opportunity to get the most out of their ability from you, their caring coach.

Without desire and commitment, even the most talented player will eventually fail or just lose interest. When talented, immature players are treated like superstars at a young age by adoring adults, the kids have been done a great disservice. Because of all this over-the-top attention and fuss about them, kids will feel like they have already accomplished their goals and the desire to get better doesn't have a chance to grow. They feel entitled, so why put out the effort? With a more balanced approach to youth baseball, where the focus is less about competition and more about an environment in which kids can have fun while learning life lessons, every kid will benefit and will be more likely to want to continue because they're having fun. Kids who have an unusual passion for the game will always find a way to pursue it on a higher level. The important thing to recognize is this: Is it the kid's passion, or is it the adult's passion? One thing is for sure. All kids have other interests that are only about having fun. When adults participate in scheduling all of a child's free time year after year just so they can win this or that World Series in their age group, kids will soon realize that they are not having fun: it's a job. When this happens, a kid's desire and commitment to baseball will fade in favor of doing something that will allow them to fulfill a once-in-a-lifetime experience: being a kid.

The Little League World Series is just one example in which the balance between a twelve-year-old's emotional makeup and the national television coverage and media hype of this event make you wonder who this is actually for: kids, or adults who see super-talented kids as entertainment. The Little League World Series appears to be a very popular attraction, and for that reason, isn't going away anytime soon. On the positive side, it's an opportunity for kids with advanced skills to go as far as they can as a twelve-year-old. When you think about it, the Olympics are no different. In figure skating and gymnastics, you see very young athletes competing on the world stage for millions of viewers to watch on television. That, in itself, is not a problem. The problem comes when parents and coaches lose perspective on an even higher level. Many parents who are watching these events on national television can't resist the notion that their child is just as talented and become motivated to push their child toward these very high goals. Their perception becomes their reality and the kids now have to live up to it, ready or not. Many coaches lose perspective by making it their mission to develop a team for the sole purpose of reaching the highest level of competition, using talented kids to fulfill their own ambitions.

It's very important for parents to separate their natural tendency toward wanting their child to be a superstar and acknowledging their child's level of interest and passion in this context. Many people have many opinions as to whether it's good or bad for youth sports to be presented in a way that promotes a very high level of competition between very young children. As a volunteer coach, it's important to keep a proper perspective about these very high levels of competition, understanding that very few athletes have all the required elements to become one of the elite. The glory that we see while watching the Little League World Series or the Olympics can negatively influence our behavior as volunteer coaches. If we use these events to point out to our young athletes what is possible when you put forth consistent good effort, however, they can be great teaching tools. Not that everyone is going to make it to the Little League World Series, but learning the life lesson that *effort leads to change in oneself* is what will help you maximize your talents as they apply to your passion, baseball or otherwise. All you can do as a coach is help each individual become the best that they can be. The problem is that, when kids are young, they will do what you say and end up trying to fulfill your unrealistic expectations if you are asking too much from them.

In martial arts we have a saying: *"Once you reach 'black belt,' you have learned to walk; now, you may begin the journey."*

This may come as a surprise to many people, because in this country the perception of attaining a "black belt" is something like what we see in the movies—people performing superhuman feats. Just beginning the journey is a concept even the student doesn't thoroughly understand until sometime after they have reached the very high goal of attaining black belt. Up until now, they have been training hard for years to perfect technique. Understandably, to them it seems like they are learning a lot, which they are. As time passes, a more complete understanding of the technique develops and the student begins to blossom as a martial artist; the seeds of the deeper life-lessons have taken root and intuition also develops. By the time a student reaches black belt in my school, they are indeed super-talented athletes who have met all the requirements of a strenuous multi-year program. They look impressive! But just like a young baseball player reaching the very high milestone known as the Little League World Series, it doesn't really mean anything unless character has been developed and life lessons learned. Adults, parents, and coaches are the ones who need to lead the way in these crucial areas of a child's development!

Those who choose to believe that reaching a goal somehow elevates them above others as a human being, lack humility and will experience their own ability to learn slowing down or even ceasing. As I write this chapter, a seven-year-old former student of mine is displaying this know-it-all attitude. He is being affected by his father's negative influence on him. This is the story of a very impatient father who seems to be living vicariously through his son, which never works out well for the child.

Grant, who is a talented, big-for-his-age seven-year-old, expressed to his teammates that if he didn't get to play first base on the all-star team, he wasn't going to play at all. Well, as it turns out, the all-star team coach picked another boy to play first base and Grant was to play left field. Grant's dad pulled him off the team. Where do you think Grant got the idea that if he didn't get his way, he wasn't going to play? Grant is already modeling his father's arrogant behavior at seven-years-old and his baseball career is on a downhill slide. Grant's father, who only sees things from his perspective, is denying his son the opportunity of the youth baseball experience. "I'll show them," he must have thought. "I'll pull my kid off the team and they'll be sorry!" The only one who will be sorry is Grant later on in his life, when he realizes that he was robbed of the opportunity to just have fun playing baseball when he was a kid. Unrealistic expectations from parents will sour kids on any activity, because the kids realize that it's supposed to be fun, but they have no say in the matter. I have seen this happen many times and it usually ends up with the child coming up with various reasons why they want to quit. They're not quite sure why they want to quit because it's confusing to a child when a parent acts this way. They just know they're not having fun.

Kids of all ages are still developing physically and maturing emotionally. Parents of these kids are often inexperienced— although some won't admit it—and will make poor decisions on behalf of their child, as did Grant's father. Coaches who understand and respect this can play a huge role in how these young athletes will perform during practice, during games, and ultimately, later in their lives. Being informed about such things as conditioning, adequate rest for pitchers, and correct instruction of mechanics is what will help young players succeed, not yelling, intimidating, and embarrassing players in front of their peers. Parents will also gain respect for your knowledge of the game and your ability to work with young players.

If your attitude is a "my way or the highway" approach, make sure you're well qualified through your own thorough research on the subject and not just feeding your own ego. If your ego is in control without the skills and knowledge to back it up, you'll be a detriment to the team instead of what you could've been if you had more knowledge: the team's best asset.

When players are young, they should be developing skills and athleticism. This is where the real success lies, not in winning the game. If you approach your volunteer coaching career with this philosophy being a priority, you'll never regret it. It doesn't mean that you're not interested in winning. It means you're interested in winning the right way by being patient and teaching kids to play the game correctly. Whatever their level of ability, kids will benefit from the *process* of skill development and will use this training in other areas of their life as well. Whether you had winning teams or not, kids will never forget you as someone who tried their best to help them. There is no greater reward for coaching than to be out in your community and to unexpectedly hear these respectful words spoken by someone from your past: Hello, Coach!

If you equate success with winning youth baseball games, you will be disappointed much of the time because you will not recognize real success—your players' personal development. The only thing you will recognize will be your players' failures. By continuing to develop skills—and depending on natural ability, desire, attitude, and work ethic—some players may end up playing in college or professionally, where success is more equated with winning. Because these players were taught the correct process of skill development at a young age, they will be well equipped with the discipline and perseverance it takes to give them a chance to succeed at this high level of play.

Some coaches tend to ignore less talented players, although they will never admit it. They do it because they feel these players can't help them win games. When winning becomes top priority for a coach, ignoring less talented players is exactly what will happen. Sure, most coaches will make an effort to get all the players in the game, but the win-at-any-cost coach will only let his so-called worst players play in the final inning when the score is 18-2 and the game is obviously won or lost. These coaches actually seem to feel good about themselves for letting everyone play. But when you see a nine-year-old kid sitting on the bench for the whole game only to get to play when there is no chance of losing or winning, you question the coach's motives. Coaches with this thoughtless approach seem to forget the players' young ages, treating them like mature adults and expecting them to "just deal with" rejection. A more correct approach to coaching young players would be to treat every one of the players on your team fairly by offering your time to help them improve because, relatively speaking, they're all beginners, talented or not. When you invest your time in helping a kid get better, you will find their strengths and you are more likely to find a way to get them in the game.

Remember, your duty as a volunteer youth coach is to motivate, teach, and inspire young athletes to be their best, not for you to be a winning coach.

By letting all your players know you are there to help them, you are giving them a choice in the matter. You will find out who wants to work for it and who wants it for nothing. If the gifted players think they don't need instruction, teach them how to ride the pine. Sitting on the bench during the game because of an arrogant attitude can really help a young player gain perspective; just be ready for the parent's response. Some parents will thank you for it; others will chastise you for it. It just depends on *their* attitude. Make your decisions on who plays where and when, based not only on a player's ability to play the position, but their personal effort and attitude. You may or may not have a winning season with this approach, but it's a winning way as it applies to your players' futures. Naturally gifted or not, without consistent good effort and good attitude, not much will be accomplished in baseball, or life.

Winning games at the expense of ignoring young players' needs is not success. Helping every player develop skill and have fun is success, whether you win or lose.

Some parents tend to ignore the fact, or can't see that their child *is* less talented and will put excessive pressure on them, make excuses for them, or blame others when their child isn't seen as "one of the best." Others understand very well the natural gift their child has and go about making sure that everyone knows it. They become like managers of their little "professional." It's not pretty. This happens a lot in youth sports. If your coaching philosophy is based on the idea that *good effort leads to getting the most out of your ability*, you will be offering training to the parents as well as to the young players; you will help parents understand what it takes to develop skill at every level of play.

Eventually, some parents may gain respect for the difficulty that their child faces when it comes to playing baseball. It's not easy. But many won't hear you because their ears are plugged when it comes to hearing the truth—that it takes time to reach your individual goals and there are no shortcuts. These things will always be a part of youth sports, but coaches should do their best to help parents understand that making excuses, blaming others, or bragging does nothing to help their child develop skill.

One of the biggest problems an inexperienced coach faces is parents who start out with the thinking that their child definitely is one of the best and is obviously on their way to Division I college baseball or the major leagues. These parents are off to a rough start as it pertains to their child's baseball journey. They are getting way ahead of themselves. It will be hard for them to have a clear vision of their child's true talents and desires because their own thinking is clouded with future results for their child. The first time you (the coach) correct their child's mechanics or attitude, you will trigger in these delusional parents an emotional response that will play itself out either right away, or worse, later. It's usually later, after they have gained support from others like themselves. Often, when they don't get the instant results that they are seeking while playing on your team, these parents will start their own travel team to accommodate their future big-leaguers. And remember those assistants who helped you in the beginning? When their child doesn't get their way, watch out for key phrases like "But we've been your biggest supporters." People who say things like this in the context of the coach not giving them their way, whether it's deserved or not, are basically saying, "You owe us." They could care less whether or not their child deserves to play a certain position or has a bad attitude. They have respect for one thing: their own self-interest.

Play your role as a parent by being a team player with the coach, reinforcing positive lessons that are being taught instead of sabotaging the coach's efforts when your child doesn't get exactly what you want.

During your coaching career, you will come across parents whose goal is to manipulate the situation, sort of like in politics. I once had a father call me and request that I not pick his son in the upcoming draft for the recreation league. He explained to me that his son, Jake, should play for Coach Smith's team because their players were of a higher caliber. "Jake needs to play with the more talented team; you understand."

I understood perfectly that Jake's father was in the business of manipulating situations for his son as he orchestrated his son's rise to stardom in baseball. Jake was a pretty good ballplayer and, in spite of a bad attitude, had a successful high school career. He went on to play at a Division II college, where he was a relief pitcher with modest success for two years until he switched colleges, looking for a better coach. The results were much the same at the new college. Every year that Jake played baseball from age six through high school, his father interfered with the process, trying to "make it happen" for Jake. The only thing he accomplished with this arrogant approach was alienating his son from his teammates. They saw Jake as a spoiled brat with a bad attitude whose father played politics with coaches. When Jake got to college, his father no longer could interfere, but the damage was done. Jake's natural talent was never developed to its highest level because his father took him down the wrong path starting at age eight when he was more focused on which team Jake was on instead of teaching Jake that having a good attitude and putting forth a good effort toward skill development is what would help him reach his goals.

It's almost a guarantee that, during your coaching career, you will encounter a parent like Jake's father. Fortunately, you will also come across parents whose goal is that their child actually learns something about the game of baseball *and* the game of life. These types of parents are the ones who keep you going in your coaching efforts in spite of the parents who only play politics. Their mind is clear to be able to see the personal skills and talents you have as a coach and a person that will benefit their child. They are not distracted by an attitude of immediate gratification and out-of-control ego.

Just as you teach players to let go of the negative events that happen in every ball game, a coach must be able to let go of the effects that a parent's negative attitude can have on them. It doesn't feel good to have a parent blame you when their child experiences failure or doesn't get their way. *If you volunteer to coach, this is going to happen.* In some years it happens more than others. It just depends on the character of the parents involved.

I have been blessed to have enjoyed several seasons in which the perspective and attitude of the parents was of a high order. But there will be years when you ask yourself "Exactly why is it that I continue to do this?" The answer to that question is this: "I have something to offer these kids in the way of proper training; it's not about me." I can honestly say that, in twenty years of coaching, there has never been a kid with whom I didn't eventually have a good player/coach relationship. The same cannot be said of certain parents. Some parents will hang on to their need for power and control and disrespect you no matter how much your efforts have benefited their child. They have made it about themselves instead of their kids and their egos will not allow them to acknowledge the truth.

Coach Effort, Not Outcome
Being a volunteer coach can be a rewarding experience and helpful to others if done right. Most people start coaching

when their kids are very young and some who stick with it eventually become excellent teachers and mentors of older, more experienced players. Your first coaching years can be challenging because of parents' unrealistic expectations and your own lack of knowledge about teaching baseball skills to kids with excessive amounts of energy and incredibly short attention spans. You must have *patience* to be an "effort over outcome" type of coach.

It takes patience to be an "effort over outcome" type of coach because developing skill requires effort over a period of time. Being patient will allow you the vision to see things correctly and the discipline to stay the course for the benefit of your players. If you don't have patience, you will likely be influenced by others who display a lack of patience—outcome-oriented parents who expect too much from kids. For example, a six-year-old kid can't throw accurately to first base just because you yell out, "C'mon, you gotta make good throws." They need instruction and correct repetitions at practice, not reprimands and pressure during games.

Play your role as a coach or parent by learning this lesson: yelling at kids is only exposing how little you really know.

It's all right to begin your career as a volunteer coach knowing very little about baseball. But if you come back year after year and don't take the time to increase your knowledge about training kids and knowing more about the strategies of the game, you won't be playing your role very well. You're likely to be an outcome-oriented coach when you know very little about what you are doing or what is going on in the game.

Pretending doesn't count.

You will be just like the kids. All you know is whether you are ahead or behind on the scoreboard. When things aren't going well, your emotions will take over, causing you to be focused on outcome only. The usual result of this poor preparation and lack of knowledge by adults is a lot of yelling at kids. You get frustrated when your team is losing and you have no idea how to turn it around with good instruction because you have not taken the time and effort to learn it yourself, so you yell.

Wear the Right Hat

It's important to understand that you do not have to learn everything there is to know about baseball all at once. If your team is made up of five and six-year-olds, you only need to know how to coach five and six-year-olds. Many coaches make the mistake of getting ahead of themselves and try to teach advanced techniques to kids whose attention span is about fifteen seconds. By teaching the appropriate techniques to the age group you are coaching, players will increase their skill and knowledge each year until one day they become an advanced player. Not only will they be a player with advanced skills, but they will be capable of teaching others because they did not skip steps along the way.

Teaching others is one of the best ways to further your own skill and knowledge. This concept was taught to me when I was in my early twenties by my martial arts instructor, (Sensei) Bob Ozman. It definitely works to deepen your own understanding and has the desirable effect of leading a young person on the path to one day becoming a very good coach themselves: in other words, a leader.

If you are a young coach starting out, I applaud you and encourage you to keep going. Sometimes it isn't easy. It can be downright disgusting when parents act like children themselves, but try to understand that just like you, they are inexperienced and they have emotions. Be patient and learn as much as you can from the wealth of material that is available these days from books and videos. Proceed with humility and be willing to learn from others with more coaching experience than you. Make sure you are wearing the right hat—the youth coach hat, not the big-league hat.

My Mentors

During my early coaching years, Jack Hand and Greg Gunnells had a profound effect on me as I paid attention to the wisdom they had to offer. Jack was thirty years my senior and founder of the Mid-State Amateur Baseball Association (MSABA) in Nashville, Tennessee. Jack was a tireless worker when it came to youth baseball and spent many long hours volunteering his time for the advancement of the sport, whether he was taking care of local ball fields or showing a kid how to swing a bat. I saw the responsibility he took as a volunteer as if it was his job. He did it for the love of the game and the benefit of kids. We had many long talks about coaching philosophy and I learned a lot from him.

Greg played a different role in my coaching career. He woke me up to the rhythm of the game.

I remember talking him into coaching with me when my son Phillip and Greg's son Clint were twelve. I wanted him to be the head coach, but he told me that he would be my assistant. I asked him if he would like to coach third base, but he said that I should do it. Coaching third base is a big responsibility and I was trying to yield to Greg's superior level of knowledge but, in his wisdom he must have thought "How is Chuck going to learn anything if I do everything?" I am thankful for that opportunity and Greg guided me through the many different strategies involved with coaching a baseball game. There is a lot to learn. When you take on the title of "Coach," you have the choice to start learning or keep pretending that you already know it all. There will be people in your midst like Jack and Greg, but you won't recognize them if you think you know it all.

Bob Ozman—My karate Sensei, Bob Ozman, was the first person to suggest to me that I could be a teacher. That was thirty five years ago. I was twenty-five-years-old. I have to admit, it had never crossed my mind to teach. I was a young, professional musician, and practicing martial arts while pursuing my career in music were my only focus. Sensei Ozman opened my eyes to the many opportunities that lie ahead through teaching others. He used to say, "If you want to really get good at something, teach it. Not only do you pass your knowledge on to others, but it benefits you as well." He was a real stickler for proper technique, but what I remember most about Sensei Ozman was the wisdom he passed on to me and his other students who taught at his dojo in Van Nuys, California.

To be an effective teacher or coach, you just have to care.
–Bob Ozman (1936–2012).

Mission Statement

Remember what is best for the kids and let your efforts show that you care about them more than your coaching career. Help every one of them to get the most out of their ability, whether they are naturally talented or not, and be willing to spend extra time with those who need it or want it. Make it your goal to affect the lives of every young player you come in contact with in a positive way that will benefit their unique needs as a ballplayer and as a person. To them, you will always be "Coach."

Chapter 19

At What Cost Are We Willing to Win?

Parents' and Coaches' Roles in Playing the Game the Right Way: make treating young players fairly a priority over winning the game.

No one is trying to lose the game. We have come to compete. We are trying to win. Trying to win is always a good goal. It drives us to get the most out of our abilities.

Youth coaches should have a second goal, however—winning the right way, by remembering that they are dealing with kids (not professional athletes), and understanding the responsibility that comes with that. Kids will generally respect what their coach or parent says because they have been taught to do that, but when the competition begins, be careful about what you are asking these young, inexperienced players to do. If your ego is in control, you're likely to lose perspective by taking on the persona of a big-league coach and you'll be trying to win with unrealistic expectations being placed on kids who are just trying to have fun.

It's human nature to want to win, and the desire to win is high at all levels of play. But under what circumstances is it the only goal?

Professional players are hired to get the job done and, ultimately, winning is the only goal. At many colleges this is also true. Coaches are hired to put together a winning team and players are expected to produce results. If they can't accomplish this goal over a period of time, they'll be replaced. Even in high school, the emphasis is on winning and a player's skills need to be honed or they won't be playing much, and might not even make the team at all. But unlike professional baseball, where winning is foremost, there are other important things to consider when coaching these younger, less mature high school players. A high school coach is still a youth coach and there are unique responsibilities that come with that. Parents of high school players also need to stay focused on their main role: raising their kids to become responsible citizens, not just baseball players. How parents and coaches play their role during competition can have an impact on how young, impressionable high-school players go about living their lives.

Many players of high-school age think they know it all, and it takes a coach with skills beyond baseball to convince them otherwise. It takes a coach who cares about their future, not just today's game, a game which ultimately means nothing. It's impossible to teach someone that which they think they already know, but some very talented players may not be getting the most out of their ability because their coach is willing to ignore their arrogant "know it all" attitude. If a player brings this attitude with them to their college team, where all the players are as good as, or better than, they are, they might be wishing that they had had a mentor earlier in their career who taught them the value of humility. If kids do not learn humility when they are young, it's only a matter of time until the world teaches it to them.

These three levels of play—professional, college, and high school—do have something in common: relatively speaking, the training period is over; either you can compete, or you can't. Unlike these advanced levels of competition, however, youth sports are the initial training period where becoming athletic, learning the basics, and developing a good attitude should be the top priority. Try to win, but do so with these goals in mind.

Even in professional baseball, there are things to be considered when it comes to the cost of winning. Big-league coaches understand the need for pitch counts and proper rest for pitchers. They're not willing to risk injury to one of their pitchers by overusing them. There are pitching coaches, experienced trainers, and a complete pitching staff to ensure that everyone stays healthy. Many colleges have these resources as well. Even though the stakes are high at these levels of play, managers and coaches make sure there is adequate time for pitchers to rest and for position players to heal after sustaining any kind of injury. Unfortunately, in youth sports, I have witnessed just the opposite many times over the years because many parents and coaches understand only one thing: winning!

When winning becomes the most important thing in youth sports, basics get skipped and teaching life lessons becomes non-existent because coaches and parents are willing to do anything to accomplish their goal of winning. When this happens, a crucial period of training for young players will pass and they don't get it back. Drills to help kids become more athletic should be the focus, instead of trick plays that will be useless in the future.

When a team of six-year-olds goes undefeated during the season, for example, it's not because they have lots of experience and have trained hard to develop their skills. Think about it; they've only been alive for six years! No, it's more likely because, for some reason, the coach was able to assemble more naturally gifted six-year-olds than the other teams had. To make matters worse, some of these coaches are over-aggressive and have their players steal bases relentlessly, totally outmatching the defensive

Coaches and Parents

If you do not take action by increasing your own knowledge of the needs of a young athlete, competition and your perspective about it will be out of balance and the kids are the ones it will affect most. Make no mistake: when the competition begins, you will be trying to win the game, which is what you should be doing, but because of your own lack of knowledge, you may be asking young kids to do things they are not physically or emotionally prepared to do. Such actions fall into the category of winning at any cost.

skills of other, less talent- kids, some of whom have never played before. The results of this self-indul- gent coaching behavior are lot of infield homeruns as the ball misses one glove after another while an outmatched team of six- year-olds tries desperately get an out. When coaches are satisfied with win- ning—with their stacked team of naturally tal- ented six-year-olds—and ignore the more sustain- able goals of teaching ba- sic skills, sportsmanship, attitude, and developing athleticism, young play- ers are the ones who lose because having a winning season as a six-year-old doesn't lead anywhere; developing skill, a good attitude, and athleticism does.

The mental and physical welfare of young athletes of all ages can get lost in the heat of competition. Many coaches and parents have very little experience and, once the competition begins, do not have the discipline to do the right thing on behalf of their young, at-risk players. When the adults who are in charge are ignorant about proper training techniques, the rules of the game, and the emotional needs of young players, you can bet that things are not going to go right. Many coaches and parents will not admit to themselves or to others their need for help in these crucial areas of youth sports. After all, doesn't admitting that you need help make you appear weak? Quite the opposite is true. *It is an admirable sign of strength to seek out instruction that will increase your knowledge and skill.* The only people who will consider you weak are those who are themselves weak.

Education for coaches and parents is the key to success in youth sports. Until rec leagues, middle schools, and high schools take action and require more knowledge on the part of their coaches, the physical and emotional needs of young players will continue to be overlooked in favor of doing anything to win. When kids have an issue such as fear, or an injury they are not sure about, telling them to "just suck it up" or using the macho standard "you gotta be tough" may backfire and have negative consequences. I have witnessed coaches leave a star player in the game after twisting an ankle, only to see him limp around on the field while there are perfectly healthy players (maybe less talented) on the bench waiting their turn. This is the "win at any cost" mentality.

Making a kid do something they are not ready for can not only shatter their confidence, but it can also lead to injury. Encouraging them to play through pain could be disastrous. Adults are the ones who need to know the difference. "Does it hurt?" or "Are you hurt?" are two different questions. When young kids get hit by the ball, have a collision with another player, or trip while running the bases, it hurts, but they're not sure if they're injured or not. Because they're young, their first reaction is to cry, which affects the emotions of adults. Letting them come out of the game after every little bump or bruise, however, will do little to boost their confidence. If they're actually injured, that's a different story; take them out. If their leg is broken, it's pretty obvious. If they get hit by the ball, it's less obvious if there's an injury. If a child's elbow or shoulder is sore from overuse, however, they may be in trouble and not realize it because it doesn't hurt that badly. Although a young player may be able to "tough it out" and play through the pain in their elbow for the sake of winning today's game, they could pay a high price in the future for something that really didn't have much value other than pleasing adults.

Here are some eye-opening statistics, according to Safe Kids USA:

- More than 3.5 million children ages 14 and under receive medical treatment for sports injuries each year.

- Injuries associated with participation in sports and recreational activities account for 21 percent of all traumatic brain injuries among children in the United States.

- Overuse injury, which occurs over time from repeated motion, is responsible for nearly half of all sports injuries to middle- and high-school students. Immature bones, insufficient rest after an injury, and poor training or conditioning contribute to overuse injuries among children.

- Most organized sports-related injuries (62 percent) occur during practices rather than games. Despite this fact, a third of parents often do not take the same safety precautions during their child's practices as they would for a game.

- A recent survey found that among athletes from ages 5 to 14, 15 percent of basketball players, 28 percent of football players, 22 percent of soccer players, 25 percent of baseball players, and 12 percent of softball players have been injured while playing their respective sports.

- Children ages 5 to 14 account for nearly 40 percent of all sports-related injuries treated in hospital emergency departments. The rate and severity of sports-related injury increases with a child's age.

Little Leaguer's elbow—medial apophysitis—frequently affects pitchers between 9 and 15 years of age. Here, on page 234, is a description and diagram of this injury from the book, *The Sports Medicine Patient Advisor,* written by Pierre Rouzier, M.D.

Little Leaguer's elbow can also affect position players who throw often without adequate rest, as is the case when young players play for more than one team during the same season, or play an excessive amount of games on a competitive travel team. Playing without adequate rest and some time off will surely lead to overuse of a young player's arm.

Play your role as a parent by being proactive and making sure that your child has a balanced approach to training, with adequate rest.

Young, inexperienced players will often say what they think their coach or parents want to hear. "I'm fine; I can pitch another inning" is just one example. If Kids are getting the message from adults that winning is the only measure of success, they will unwittingly risk injury to their arm in order to fulfill the unrealistic expectations of adults, and will play through the pain in their elbow. Playing through pain in your elbow is not okay. When a young player is hit by the baseball, however, they may think that they are injured because it hurts so much when, in fact, it's usualjust a temporary sting. Just making eye contact with them will cause them to reach out to you by crying. They're scared, and they want you to reassure them that they are okay. In this case, it can be difficult to convince them to stay in the game, even though they're not actually injured.

What is Medial Apophysitis (Little Leaguer's elbow)?

Little Leaguer's elbow is pain on the side of the elbow that is closest to the body.

The elbow joint is made up of the bone in the upper arm (humerus) and one of the bones in the lower arm (ulna). The bony bumps at the end of the humerus are called epicondyles. The bump closest to the body is called the medial epicondyle, and the bump on the outer side of the elbow is called the lateral epicondyle.

The muscles that work to bend the wrist attach at the medial epicondyle, and the muscles that work to straighten the wrist attach at the lateral epicondyle. Too much bending of the wrist will irritate the muscles that attach to the medial epicondyle.

In a child, the bones grow from areas called growth plates. There is a growth plate at the medial epicondyle called the medial apophysis. In Little Leaguer's elbow this growth plate is irritated or inflamed.

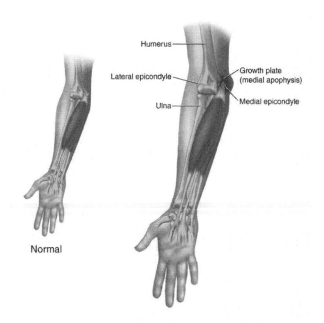

As a coach or parent, be responsible and inform yourself about these issues *before they happen* on behalf of your young athletes. In the big leagues, a player will often be the one who decides whether or not he's ready to play after a minor injury; a young, inexperienced player cannot be expected to do that.

Competition can influence people in a negative way. Coaches and parents who are obsessed with winning may lose awareness of the wellbeing of their players. Football players receiving multiple concussions is a particularly disturbing trend. Players are encouraged or even required by their coach to be physically tough if they expect to play. There is nothing wrong with that, but many young players who have had a concussion will be willing to play before they are totally healed. Some players may get too tough for their own good. They want to impress their coach, but are not knowledgeable about the lasting effects of recurring concussions. If the coach allows them to play, they are placing their player's health at risk! All coaches should be aware of injuries that are common to their sport and take measures to safeguard the wellbeing of their athletes.

In the heat of competition, this takes strong mental discipline. The urge to win is mighty in all of us.

The physical and mental health of young athletes is more important than the egos and unrealistic expectations of parents and coaches!

As a parent, it feels great when your child is successful, but this feeling can cloud the mind when it comes to proper training. It's easy to equate success with winning only, but this is not helpful to a nine-year-old. It might be useful for a professional, who has learned to motivate himself to work harder to achieve the reality that at their level, success is equated to winning. A young player is still learning this life lesson: *that there is more to success than winning a ball game.* It's the responsibility of the adults in their lives to teach this to young players. Understanding what *real* success is can help.

In the book *The Mental Game of Baseball*, authors H.A. Dorfman and Karl Kuehl write this description: "If you want success, you prepare for success. You expect success. And in your pursuit, you are winning!" For parents, there is a natural tendency to want kids to be successful all the time and never experience failure. But when a coach or parent uses their grown-up skills to manipulate situations so their kids can have *feel-good* success, it'll deprive them of a very important part of their baseball journey: the need to travel the road themselves and experience the bumps.

Play your role as a parent by helping your child understand that preparation and proper training will teach them how to negotiate the bumps along the way on their baseball journey and in their life as a whole.

When parents interrupt the learning process by seeking quick fixes and ignoring proper training concepts, it means that they just can't wait for success. For them, proper training takes too long; they want their child to have success right now, ready or not. The result of parents putting too much pressure on their child to succeed, or blaming others because they can't stand to see their child fail is this: Their child will pay for it in the future because they will not be able to compete with other players who took the time to develop their skill and athleticism, players whose parents correctly understood *their* role early on in the process.

Keep in mind what's best for the kids, not what's best for you or the other adults!

At younger ages, proper instruction is essential. It pays for coaches and parents to learn as much as they can about the game and the skills needed to have success. If they do, they will coach in a responsible manner and actually teach kids real baseball strategy and technique. This is a winning way! Instead, many youth baseball coaches spend their time learning despicable techniques to win that only amount to an adult coach taking advantage of the opposing team's young, inexperienced players.

One of the worst "win at all costs" plays that I have witnessed is a coach sending his nine-year-old runners home from third base after the pitch when the catcher is simply throwing the ball back to the pitcher. As soon as the ball leaves the catcher's hand, the coach yells go and the runner takes off. This has nothing to do with the real game of baseball, and in the case of older, more experienced players, the runner would be out every time; the pitcher would simply throw the ball back to the catcher, who, in turn, tags the hopeless runner out. But when a kid is nine-years-old and it's his first year as a pitcher, he's nervous and is having a hard enough time just getting the ball over the plate. He does not have the composure to defend against such a play. This is exactly why some youth coaches will do it. Win at all costs! After being surprised (by this thoughtless coach's behavior), the young, inexperienced pitcher usually throws the ball away as he rushes his throw to get the runner out and the coach now feels like a genius because he helped his team score another run.

Adults who use win-at-any-cost techniques against kids are more like bullies than coaches. They are only concerned with winning and are not interested in teaching kids how to play the game properly. Plays like the one mentioned earlier are very irresponsible and the only reason they work is because the young players have not had enough time and experience to measure up to the opposing coach's win-at-any-cost tactics. Coaches who use these tactics set up a snowball effect of negative behavior for the rest of the game. If the coach for the opposing team responds with the same thoughtless behavior, the real game of baseball gets lost while the gamesmanship of adults takes over.

Another unfortunate result of this negative style of coaching is this: When the coach on the opposing team is more responsible and refuses to reciprocate by intimidating young, inexperienced pitchers, his team will probably lose the game because of those *cheap* runs. Now, the responsible coach is criticized by parents on his own team for "not being able to win the close ones" or some other unenlightened reason.

Many excellent coaches have decided to "hang it up" because they grow weary of dealing with parents' unrealistic expectations and instant gratification attitudes. Win-at-any-cost type coaches tend to stick around because many parents have adopted that same attitude; these coaches have a built-in support system. A winning coach is popular regardless of how they accomplish winning because many parents think that the only definition of success is winning a game. Once again, understand that when the game starts, that competitive spirit will get in us, and how we as adults deal with it will determine whether the kids have a positive experience or a negative experience. For kids, winning games will be a truly positive experience only if they were taught to win the right way and were treated with fairness by responsible adults, adults who have an awareness of emotional and physical needs of young players.

The more we know about the game and our athletes' physical and emotional makeup, the better prepared we will be to make good decisions on their behalf. If kids are taught the proper way to train and win at an early age, instead of having adults manipulate outcomes, make excuses for them when they fail, or overlook their bad behavior because they're talented, they'll see the benefits later. The kids will gain an understanding that developing sustainable baseball skills requires consistent and correct training over time. When parents and coaches interfere with that process by ignoring poor behavior, manipulating outcomes, and making excuses, *they're trying to win at the expense of a child's development.*

Here are some examples that I have experienced in the past of winning at any cost. The team was a group of fourteen-year-old boys with average ability. One of our better pitchers, James, was removed from the game after reaching his pitch count, but more importantly, we could see fatigue setting in as we watched his delivery. After the game in a discussion with all the parents about the next game in the tournament, James' dad asked why we took his son out of the game. I explained why and his only comment, in an angry tone of voice, was, "This is baseball; you gotta be tough!"

It's this kind of attitude and lack of education on the part of parents and coaches that eventually will lead to serious arm injury for a young player who is asked to pitch with a fatigued or overused arm.

The next day, when we didn't start his son as a pitcher, the father was even angrier, and for the rest of the season, disrespected the very coaches who had his son's best interests at heart. James' dad was seemingly clueless that a pitching arm needs rest, but also was unwilling to trust experienced coaches. In an effort to satisfy his own ego, instant gratification and winning became so important to him that he was blinded to the fact that his son needed proper rest before pitching again. The cost for this ignorant behavior on the part of the father will be high if he continues to make it about himself instead of his son.

In another season, with nine-year-old players, we had a boy named Kyle who was one of our more talented players and a very good pitcher. We were in a competitive league against some very good teams. It was clear from the beginning that we would not win many games mainly due to the fact that it was our first year as a team, and many of the other teams were in their fourth season together. Kyle's dad decided to have him play on a rec team as well, trying to have the best of both worlds. On one hand, you get to experience some tough competition. On the other hand, you get to win more games because it's the recreational league and the competition is not as tough.

Since Kyle was a talented pitcher, however, he was naturally being used by both teams. Playing for two teams poses many problems, but the worst thing was that Kyle ended up with a sore elbow on several occasions and ended up in the dugout instead of the game.

What happened next boggles the mind. Whenever Kyle was taken out or took himself out of the game because his elbow was sore, his dad would take him outside the dugout and play catch with him to "check his arm out" and try to convince him that he was okay to play. On one occasion I overheard him tell Kyle that he was okay to go out and play shortstop, but to just throw it softly over to first. Both of his parents would continually come over to the dugout and ask him, "Are you sure you don't want to play?" whenever their son was sitting out because his elbow was sore. To satisfy their own feelings of pride, they seemed willing to take a chance on a more serious injury by talking Kyle into playing through the pain in his elbow. They, like James' dad, were in denial about the fact that overuse of a pitching arm can lead to some serious trouble down the road. It will only be a matter of time until there is a real problem with the health of their child's arm if these parents do not start playing their role correctly. They need to be informed about the importance of rest for a pitching arm, realizing that the real success is not winning the current game that they are playing, but helping their child to develop slowly and safely as they continue on their baseball journey.

The Tortoise and the Hare
Another common mistake in youth sports is the thinking that only the naturally gifted players can help you win games. Who these naturally gifted players are is also somewhat up for debate when you have inexperienced coaches and self-serving parents.

Focusing only on the so-called "best players" is a win-at-any-cost attitude and is unfair to any young player who shows excellent effort and attitude. Here is one example of where, I as a coach, was criticized by certain parents on the team for not being able to win the close ones because of who was playing first base.

We had assembled a group of nine-year-old players to compete in a travel league. There were some different levels of natural ability and attitude among the players, but I felt that through proper training and effort, all of them could improve upon their individual weaknesses and eventually become competitive. As it turns out, we had two players who shared playing first base: Ian and Ben. Some of our parents had coached in previous years and had experience with both boys. These parents and others, whom they influenced, had very definite opinions about each boy's role on the team.

Ian (the tortoise) did not possess a high level of natural athletic ability. Because of this, some of the parents already had decided that he "just didn't have what it takes" to be a good ballplayer. When I would work with Ian on certain mechanical faults during practice, these parents and former volunteer coaches would comment that "we've tried to get him to overcome that and it won't happen." At nine-years-old, these adults had already given up on Ian, which basically tells you something about their own level of expertise as it applies to being a youth coach. What they failed to realize is that, while Ian did lack natural athletic ability, he possessed a very high level of desire, respect, and perseverance. He also was fortunate to have supportive parents with a realistic perspective.

Because of these very desirable traits, Ian was getting the most out of his ability and was moving forward on his journey to becoming a better ballplayer. The naysayers couldn't see it because they had already decided that Ian wasn't very good, and because of their lack of knowledge, that's where their perception of him remained.

Unlike Ian, Ben (the hare) was naturally athletic. The parents on our team who had previously coached Ian had also coached Ben before. They could see his natural talent, but were also somewhat aware of attitude issues with Ben. As is often the case with talented players, however, these parents were willing to overlook Ben's poor attitude because of his talent. When it came to playing first base, Ben, because of his natural ability, just assumed that he knew how to do it, so our instruction did not sink in. He lacked humility, a result of his parents' own attitude and the special treatment he received from others, so his mind was not open to constructive criticism. Ian, on the other hand, listened to our every word and learned the position well. Over time, Ian *became* a first baseman; Ben did not. Still, I was criticized whenever Ian played first base because certain parents had decided that Ian just wasn't very good and Ben was, due to the previous assessment of their individual physical abilities.

Ian's and Ben's ultimate success at the position was similar. Ian was successful because he had worked hard to learn the position and other techniques to help him overcome some lack of ability. Ben had some success because he had natural ability, but did very little to actually learn the position. My prediction over time is that, if Ian is fortunate enough to have more coaches who value his effort, he's on the path to becoming a very good first baseman with sustainable skills. Ben may have temporary success because of his natural ability, but because of his and his parents' arrogant attitude, he will eventually realize the consequences of this negative behavior. What I realized through this experience was that the difference between Ian's attitude and Ben's directly reflects the attitudes of their parents.

When trying to win the game, you have to show confidence in players who give their best effort for the team. *This is winning the right way; it's fair.* A gifted player is of little use to the team when he doesn't pay attention and is just relying on his undeveloped talent to get the job done. To cave in as a coach and put Ian on the bench and Ben on first base just because some parents feel that Ben (never mind his poor attitude) is the better player, would be a huge mistake for the team and an injustice to Ian and Ben. It represents trying to "win at all costs" by being unfair to Ian and ignoring his good effort and attitude, and failing to teach Ben an important life lesson: that receiving special treatment because of natural ability only leads to eventual failure because of lack of humility. In this example, Ian deserves to play first base and Ben needs an attitude adjustment!

Often in life, the persistent tortoise wins over the lazy and overconfident hare.

A big problem in youth baseball arises when a gifted player makes a great play once in a while and then is perceived as the most valuable player, even though he often misses the routine plays due to lack of effort, humility, or poor technique. Since a higher percentage of plays are actually routine, this is a recipe for failure. People tend to put talented players on a pedestal because of their natural ability and are willing to ignore poor attitude and effort. If we are going to win, we should do it with the players who show respect and give the proper effort! Regardless of natural ability or not, having respect and giving a good effort is a choice every player can make.

The interesting thing to note in the tortoise-and-hare example is that, whether our team was winning or losing the games, it had very little to do with who was playing first base. Still, the win-at-any-cost mentality was alive and well when certain parents were advocating setting Ian on the bench in favor of the more talented Ben, even though Ben remained clueless as to how to play the position. Misconceived perception on the part of parents and coaches leads to injustice for kids, whether they are like the tortoise *or* the hare. The result of this lack of awareness is this: Kids who have less ability, but are working hard to overcome it, are rewarded with a trip to the bench, while the more gifted player is getting the wrong message that it's his talent that will get him where he wants to go, not his effort. We lost games that season because our team was not making routine defensive plays, but the opponents were. Several of our players had not put in enough time to become consistent on basic throwing and catching skills. This is where the real story was, but instead of taking responsibility for the fact that they had not practiced enough with their kids on the basics, many parents put the blame on the coach for playing a kid whom they thought had no talent, such as Ian.

The cost of winning is too high when we overuse a young player's pitching arm only to satisfy the various needs of adults. The cost of winning is too high when a young player is overlooked during games because he was labeled an untalented player during tryouts, but has worked hard and is overcoming this obstacle; the only problem is that the coach is just not creative enough to see it. We should be trying to win the game, but we should be doing it by using our real knowledge about baseball and our team's makeup. If coaches, whether they're volunteer parent coaches or coaches for hire, go on the field unprepared and just "wing it," they'll be likely to make the same mistakes over and over based on their lack of knowledge. They will overuse players who have some natural ability and sometimes even be willing to overlook bad attitudes. Players who do not possess as much natural ability will be underused, even if they are improving due to their natural drive, ambition, and good attitude. Many coaches just don't see the improvement, or refuse to see it. They want success now in the form of a win and are not interested in the concept of helping all the players become winners over time through proper effort and training.

Sometimes, small steps in a struggling player's progress go unnoticed and they end up not playing much because of it. Either the coach is inexperienced and just doesn't see the progress, or he is unwilling to be patient enough to take the time to teach these less gifted players and help them develop their skills. So when the game is on the line and the coach is more concerned with winning, he has no confidence in the less gifted player (the tortoise) because he has not personally invested any time in helping him. As a coach, he has not been paying attention to the progress of the tortoise, and these players will be underestimated and passed over. He'll go to the gifted player (the hare) every time because he knows that he has the talent. The problem is that, if he's like the hare in Aesop's fable, the gifted player will have gone to sleep in his training and his natural ability will not mean much.

If every player on the team had equal talent and a great at-titude, the job of the coach would be very easy. One could just play them all for an equal amount of minutes. In reality, it's never that way. There are always talent differences and attitude issues to deal with. Learning to balance this dynamic for the fairness of the players is a coach's challenge. If you are a youth coach, do away with misconceived perceptions and pay close attention to *all* the players' individual abilities, attitude, work ethics, and respect or lack of respect. Learn to see what is hap-pening "right now" and proceed with fairness to all players according to their effort. That way, you'll feel that you can win with your whole team the right way, and not be willing to "win at all costs."

Chapter 20

Hitting

A Parent's Role in Helping Their Kids Become Proficient at Hitting: teach kids that it's what they do before they swing that counts.

Achieving success as a hitter means something different for every player. The challenge of sustaining that success is the same for every player. It's a constant struggle, no matter how talented or how old you are.

Hitting a baseball is one of the most difficult things to do in all of sports. Just ask a big-leaguer who is experiencing the nightmare of a 0 for 25 slump. Sure, it's easy to hit the ball hard during batting practice, or hit the long ball during the home-run derby, but game time brings different challenges. When there is a formidable pitcher on the mound and the pressures of the situation are dominating a player's experience, the dynamic changes. You need to be able to react in a split second. When an experienced player goes into a slump, it's not like they forgot the hitting mechanics of the swing.

No, it's more likely that a mental issue is causing the mechanics of the swing to be less than perfect, which is a recipe for failure when you have less than one half-second to react once the ball leaves the pitcher's hand. It's very challenging at this high level to stay consistent mentally and physically throughout the season. Relatively speaking, it's no different for a young kid as they make the journey from Little League through high school. Kids face an additional obstacle, however—the lack of perspective that many adults have when it comes to competition in youth sports. There can be many reasons for this lack of perspective, but here are a few: lack of knowledge, lack of patience, lack of humility, and lack of caring. These problems must be addressed first! *When adults are able to play their role correctly, hitting a baseball becomes a lot easier for a young kid.*

Kids are still developing their skills and mental perspective of the game. They're just beginning their journey and, if they're allowed to take each step, mastering basics in proper time and order, they will develop normally. When parents and coaches interfere with the process by demanding too much too soon, excessive pressure is added and striking out feels more like a personal failure to a kid, instead of a normal part of competition.

When we want something quickly, we are likely to skip steps easily.

Preparation Is a Choice

When learning to hit a baseball, there is a logical path to follow for a young hitter. The young hitter doesn't know this path. Adults must be prepared to show it to them. Kids, or any beginner for that matter, just see a ball and they swing at it with whatever natural motion feels right to them. Without instruction, some kids do okay; others are not close. Natural athletic ability plays a role. Either way, the only focus is on hitting the ball, with little or no regard to proper preparation. Just as in the rest of life, however, there are choices to make. If we don't prepare, failure will be allowed to play too large a role and progress will be slow, or nonexistent; success will elude us. Poor preparation leads to poor results and kids will continue with this blind approach unless someone intervenes and shows them the way. It's not just the physical way to hit the ball, but the way to make choices that will increase their chance for success: choices such as proper attitude and preparation that will help them sustain success throughout the season and year to year as they grow through their experience on the baseball field.

If kids have an interest, they will listen and learn. It's just that simple. When we have a genuine interest in something, it's a lot easier to sustain the effort needed to accomplish a difficult goal. If kids have little interest, however, they will have trouble focusing because intuitively they know that they will be unable to endure this ongoing process of repeating correct motions over and over, *especially if their parents or coaches are impatient.* A good instructor—who doesn't have to be a professional—can make a difference, sometimes creating an interest in a young player, but there are other factors that will play a role in determining who continues on and who drops out. It's convenient to lay it all on the kid by saying that "they're just not interested," but pressure from overbearing parents, lack of proper instruction, unrealistically long summer seasons, and thoughtless, win-at-any-cost coaches who act like drill sergeants are more likely to cause a kid to quit prematurely than an initial lack of interest.

Most kids get way ahead of themselves from the very first swing, attempting advanced techniques while having never mastered the basics. It's like they are prepared to be unprepared. When first working with a seven-year-old, for example, putting the ball on a tee for them to hit can be an eye-opening experience. If you don't get out of the way quickly or tell them to wait, some of them will just swing wildly and you'll be dodging a bat! They don't even see you there; they just want to hit the ball. What we need to do is take that desire to hit the ball and add a process to it that will allow a young hitter to get the most out of their natural ability, whatever that is.

What is that process?

For a beginner, the process starts out the same no matter what the age: *master the basics, one step at a time.* As skill develops, the process continues with *reviewing* the basics and learning more advanced techniques. It's neverending. If you think about it, it's no different for any of us when we attempt something new, especially in sports. We have seen those who are more experienced do it and they make it look easy. When we try to mimic them, it doesn't go so well because we try to do the whole motion just like they do, but we're doing it without having mastered the basics; we don't even know what the basics are. Until we become proficient at the basic technique, our bodies are out of control. The basics are like the foundation of the house. The foundation must be built first and built correctly so that the rest of the structure can rely on it to hold things together.

To become consistent at hitting, it's what you do before you swing that counts: your mental and physical preparation. I have a simple drill that I use at my hitting school that illustrates this concept very well: the six-ball tee drill. At the beginning of every lesson, whether the student is advanced or a beginner, I have them hit six balls off of a batting tee with a good, hard swing like they would use in a game. Seems simple enough. I don't say anything during these six swings so that I can get a true gauge of a hitter's development.

Everyone thinks that they can hit these six balls successfully, but rarely is that the case. For the beginner the goal becomes hitting the ball, not the tee, or to not miss the ball entirely. For the advanced hitter, the goal is to hit six line drives. Although it's impossible to be perfect in a ball game, I let my students know that it *is* possible to become perfect or near perfect in this case. The ball is just sitting there. It doesn't move. I ask them, "During these six swings, what's the only thing that can change?" The answer is always the same: "*Me.*"

Now, imagine if that same ball was moving toward you from fifty or sixty feet away and you had to be able to tell its location and how fast it was going. Not to mention distractions such as an excited crowd or the pressure kids feel to succeed from parents and coaches. If a player hasn't perfected their swing off the batting tee where location and speed are not a factor, it's going to be very frustrating trying to hit a moving ball that gets to them very fast. Having the discipline to start with the same balanced stance before each swing and maintaining that balance throughout the swing is especially crucial when the ball is doing something different each time. Players who don't understand this are often confused as to why they aren't having success. Parents who don't understand why their kid is failing have a tendency to blame others. Most people who are in the habit of skipping the basics have all kinds of excuses as to why they are failing. I've heard lots of them, enough to fill a whole chapter. Mastering the basics is the quickest way to become proficient at hitting! It starts with the batting tee.

Play your role as a parent or coach by learning the basics, so that you can teach them to kids correctly.

If mental focus is achieved before each swing, you will have success six times out of six. Mental focus means that your body, feet, and hands act without your doing anything in your mind. You're on automatic and the mechanics you have been taught, *and have practiced*, will work for you. When thoughts are allowed to creep into the mind, mental focus is lost. The mind must remain clear. As you can imagine, this is not easy to do. But at all levels of play, it makes the difference between success and failure. Without proper mental preparation, thinking too much will become part of the process, causing tightness. Reaction time will be slower, rhythm and timing will be off, and you are leaving your fate to chance. When a player is consciously mindful of hitting the ball, they are not acting in a normal mindset, but one that is affected by inaccurate thoughts, and they will miss. What is meant by "acting in a normal mindset?" The best analogy that I can think of is riding a bike. You just get on the bike and go! You can do this successfully every time and without thought because you have done it so many times before. It feels normal. Swinging a bat to hit a baseball must feel as normal as riding a bike.

You don't think about riding the bike; you don't think about hitting the baseball. The only way this can happen successfully on a consistent basis is through consistent training!

What must be remembered is this: kids have one goal in mind and that is to have fun. So, there should be an element of fun in the training. We can't train a seven-year-old kid as though he is an adult. With this in mind, the first thing that a young player must do is learn proper swing mechanics. Without them, they won't hit six line drives off of that tee in a million years. They'll stare at that ball until their mind has almost frozen them in place and then swing wildly, hitting the tee, barely hitting the ball, or missing it entirely. As mentioned earlier, being able to hit the ball and not the tee is a good, realistic goal to start with when teaching a young, inexperienced hitter. It's also more fun! Teaching balance and keeping the head still, with the forehead coming down, eyes looking down the barrel as their bat makes contact with the ball, is the first step. Once they can accomplish this on a consistent basis, they will hit the ball and not the tee. Later, when they have gained confidence, you can teach them more advanced techniques and hitting line drives will be the goal. Challenge kids on a consistent basis and, when they fail, be prepared to help them learn from the experience.

Preparation is the key to being consistent: both "past preparation" and "preparation in the moment." The ultimate goal of preparation is to prepare the mind and body to be able to execute the learned mechanics.

In the six-ball tee drill, a player increases their chance for success if they go through the pre-swing preparation each time before swinging. This is preparation "in the moment." The longer they train, the more the correct motions will accumulate in them. In time, the player can rely on muscle memory to supply the correct motion needed not only for the six-ball tee drill, but also during competition. Also, over time, mental preparation will become a habit. This is the result of "past preparation." The two go hand in hand. One without the other is a careless approach and a good opponent will take advantage of it. During a game, a player must stay "in the moment" and can't afford to skip the preparation before each swing because it's a guarantee that a good pitcher is going through his preparation before each pitch. In a real game, "near perfect" rarely happens, even with excellent preparation. In fact, getting three hits out of ten tries is considered outstanding at high levels of play. Also, in a ball game, it must be remembered that not only should our preparation be excellent, but we must give credit to the pitcher as well.

In martial arts, which I also teach, we bow to our opponent before sparring to show respect. Our goal is to defeat them, and because we respect their ability, we rise to the task; we do not underestimate them. All fear disappears because we respect our own ability as well. The many hours of training over a long period of time are what we now trust. The feeling we have is that *we know we will succeed.* I train all my baseball players to adopt this same philosophy as it applies to hitting a baseball. Expect success! Once respect is established in our mind and we have finished the pre-swing preparation, it's time to remove all unwanted thoughts from our mind and let our training take over, allowing the pitcher to become part of our swing as we attempt to sync our timing with his. This can be the hardest thing to do. Self-doubt creeps in. "What if's" and "I gotta's" are ready to sabotage our thinking and sincerest efforts. Our thoughts take us to the future instead of allowing us to remain "in the moment."

Whenever I ask a young, inexperienced player what they are thinking while in the batter's box, they always say, "Hit the ball." This competitive thought usually causes them to lose control in their mind. They forget their preparation, and they over-swing. Loss of balance and not seeing the ball well are the results. A more useful thought would be "*see* the ball." You already know that you want to hit the ball. You knew it before you got to the game. Now it's time to *see it*. See it out of the pitcher's hand. The sooner you see the ball, the more time you have to react to its location and speed. If you have trained properly, you have a chance to hit it.

Once the player steps into the batter's box, it's time for coaches and parents to stop instructing and just be cheerleaders. Instruction with regard to technique should happen at practice. During games, any teaching should focus on attitude, sportsmanship, and effort. Too much technical instruction during games just causes players to think too much. Thinking too much makes a hitter lose their mental focus; they won't see the ball well because it takes their thoughts to the future (outcomes), letting the present moment pass them by.

As a side note, in the big leagues, it takes a 90-mile-an-hour fastball less than *one half-second* to reach the batter once it leaves the pitcher's hand. That's like the blink of an eye! For kids, there is more time to react to the ball, but lack of experience more than compensates and weak results can be expected if the mental focus is not there.

For Older, More Advanced Players
Since overthinking causes tightness, you're not quick, and a good pitcher will win every time! Instead of being part of your swing, he dominates your swing. The secret to success is to be able to control the mind, to make it free from thought.

Bruce Lee, one of the best martial artists of all time, puts it this way: *"Empty your mind. Be formless, shapeless—like water. If you put water into a cup, it becomes the cup. You put water into a bottle, it becomes the bottle. You put it into a teapot, it becomes the teapot. Now, water can flow or it can crash. Be water, my friend."*

The idea is to relax. Worrying about an outcome, such as hitting the ball, will add pressure and anxiety, causing disconnect between you and the pitcher. Clear the mind and let your training work for you as you sync your timing with the pitcher's timing, giving yourself a chance to react to whatever he throws. Become one with him. Learn to flow with good rhythm and crash at the point of contact. Do it by taking a breath before each swing and replacing unwanted thoughts with these three words: see the ball. Free the mind so that it does not stop and linger anywhere, allowing the eyes to see the ball come right out of the pitcher's hand!

And now we have to ask ourselves "Is there any training to rely on?" As coaches, have we prepared our players for success by learning what we can and passing it on to our players? Or, do we think we know it all and hide behind the more naturally talented kids to get the job done (win at any cost)? Unfortunately, know-it-all coaches who know very little are very common in youth baseball and other youth sports as well. Coaches who lack knowledge have no idea what to do with a kid who has limited athletic ability, so these players often end up on the bench much of the time while winning becomes top priority, using the so-called "best players." Being obsessed with winning becomes a sickness that affects the whole team. A much healthier approach is to be aware of your role as a youth coach, learning as much as you can about the basics of hitting and remembering that every kid can be helped to improve. Every kid! It just takes caring on the part of the adults in their life. And when it comes to hitting a baseball—one of the hardest things to do in sports—caring enough by taking the time to teach *all* kids proper and appropriate mechanics for their age is what is required. There are many good books written on the subject of hitting a baseball. One of my favorites is Charley Lau's *The Art of Hitting 300.*

Without preparation, the simplest tasks become impossible to achieve.

A ball just sitting on a tee, daring you to hit it, will win the battle if your physical and mental preparation is poor. *The ball is prepared to be hit; are you prepared to hit it?* This simple statement is a metaphor for all areas of life and crucial for success in baseball. Unfortunately, at many youth baseball parks, lack of preparation is exactly what you see and frustration is what you get. Many kids, when they are struggling, find it impossible to turn it around, no matter what you say as an instructor, because another voice in their head is speaking louder: the frustrated voice of a parent or coach. Kids feel pressure to please the adults and this can affect their performance. Sometimes this pressure is brought on by themselves for no other reason than that they are young and inexperienced. Other times, by our own exuberant behavior, innocent or not, we cause kids to try too hard to please us and the results are always the same: failure. Teaching kids to be less concerned with the outcome and more concerned with effort is beneficial because it frees them to be in the moment, not worrying about what others think. When kids are able to do this, it allows them to trust their training and enjoy the process, which will lead to a better result. They'll be having fun! The only way which we as adults will allow kids this freedom, however, is to be informed ourselves, confident that the technique we are teaching is correct, and knowing that it takes time for skill and mental awareness to develop.

Hitting Preparation Basics

- *Proper stance.* Without a balanced stance throughout the swing sequence, many things can go wrong. The rest of the hitting mechanics will be impossible to achieve and the timing will be off. For a young player, a stance about as wide as their bat is long is a good place to start, feet pointing toward the plate, weight focused on the front part of the foot (never on the heels).

- *Plate coverage.* Now that stance has been achieved, bend at the waist and knees and reach across to touch the outside of the plate with the end of the bat. This will achieve three things: plate coverage, loosening the body, weight on the balls of the feet.

- *Breathing.* While maintaining stance, bring the bat back to the shoulder, hands just below the shoulder, remaining loose. Take a breath and exhale. This will relax the shoulders and focus the mind.

- *Weight back.* From a balanced stance, with the weight evenly distributed, sit back slightly to put 60% of the weight on the back leg without letting the upper body change, other than the front shoulder slightly down and in. At this point the hands can come away from the body slightly, not too far. You are now prepared to swing.

Once learned, the pre-swing preparation takes only a couple of seconds and happens without thought. It should be performed before each swing. This takes discipline for a young player because, as mentioned earlier, all they want to do is swing, not prepare. To reinforce this in a student, I don't even put the ball on the tee until I see perfect preparation. This way, I am teaching them how to prepare, which is what they don't want to do on their own. They are then ready to hit the ball, which is what they want to do.

Remember that they are preparing for that one moment when they are ready to swing, so teach them to not linger and study the ball on the tee. Waiting too long will only cause them to tighten up. Once prepared, they should swing without thought. During a game it's tougher because the pitcher (older age groups) is attempting to throw the batter's timing off. The goal of the batter is to be prepared at the right moment so as to pick up on the pitcher's timing. Not easy. You have to stay loose. Your pre-swing routine will help you do this. When you watch a big-league player, they all have a specific pre-swing routine, which mentally prepares them. They do it the same every time and if we think about it, we could mimic our favorite player's pre-swing routine easily.

After this initial preparation—which should precede every swing—you are ready for the load and stride. This is where timing with the pitcher is achieved. The hands are back or go back before the swing. In the very beginning, when they are young, kids tend to have too much movement already, so it's beneficial to keep it simple and have the player swing from the position right where they left their hands after the initial preparation, close to the shoulder. Later on, they can load up by moving their hands back slightly with an easy motion and then forward to the path of the ball. The hands will be back and the ball of the front foot will touch down (or just press down) at the same time. At this point, the shoulder is still closed. Next, the front heel will come down and the hips will turn, bringing the hands inside (close to the body) and, as quickly as possible, to the path (height) of the ball. With the turning of the hips, the weight will shift from the back leg to a stiff front leg as the back heel comes up. It's important to remember that the hands can't move forward until the front foot touches down and hip rotation begins. The hips will bring the hands toward the path of the ball. Releasing the barrel and arm extension follow as you make contact with the ball and then follow through as the barrel continues around to the shoulder blades.

We are all familiar with baseball growing up, so on some level we may think we know how to hit a ball, until we try it for ourselves. Doing so can be beneficial. It will allow you to experience the difficult task the kids are facing. You may find out that you are just like the kids. You will only be concerned with hitting the ball and proper preparation will be absent. After you miss a few times or hit the ball poorly, you try harder but it gets worse. Trying harder without proper knowledge of the task usually sends you farther in the wrong direction no matter what you're doing. If you can't demonstrate something or at least thoroughly explain it, you can't teach it. You'll only confuse the person you're trying to teach. Practicing and learning the mechanics yourself so that you can teach can be a lot of fun and very rewarding. Having an experienced instructor teach your child is very beneficial if it's not something that you want to do or think that you can do. When trying to hit a baseball, if your child has to rely on luck, their efforts will produce weak results and it won't be long until their interest declines.

Often, when kids experience failure, the only instruction they receive is to try harder. This advice usually results in more body movement, not less, because they are not efficient with their movement, which is why they failed in the first place. Usually, the first thing to move too much is the head. Many kids will tilt their head sideways as they over-swing, bringing their ear toward the shoulder. This makes it harder for the eyes to track the ball. When hitting a baseball, the body and especially the head, must remain still as we swing. Not completely still, obviously, because the forehead must come down so that your eyes can see the ball into the hitting zone, but without unnecessary movement, tilting your head sideways.

The head should be upright with the chin going from shoulder to shoulder. Maybe a better way to put it is to maintain good and correct posture much like a dancer, gymnast, or martial artist. You must be able to pick up the ball early, right out of the pitcher's hand, and see it into the hitting zone with the forehead coming down, eyes looking down the barrel as the ball hits the bat. This is the information a young kid needs, not just "try harder."

After we have completed proper preparation, we are ready to swing, not before. Unlike a big-leaguer, a dominant pitcher is not an issue for a six or seven-year-old kid. In fact, the pitcher in this case is either an accurate machine or a coach who is aiming at their bat. Not being prepared is the number one problem for kids who are trying to become consistent at hitting a baseball. If they haven't been practicing a proper routine to use in preparation before each swing, they won't be able to rely on this crucial element of hitting during the game. Their stance, hand position, head position, body position, balance, and timing will be slightly different for each swing, just enough to make them miss the ball much of the time.

Practicing preparation over a period of time (past preparation) by preparing before each and every swing (preparation in the moment) is what will bring eventual success as a player travels on their baseball journey.

They will come to trust it.

They will have learned that *it is what you do before you swing that counts.*

Bibliography

Bagonzi, Dr. John. *The Act of Pitching*. Woodsville, NH: Pitching Professor Publications, 2001

Berra, Yogi. *The Yogi Book*. New York: Workman Publishing, 1998

Cluck, Bob. *Play Better Baseball*. Chicago: Contemporary Books, 1993

Coleman, Gene. *52-Week Baseball Training*. Champaign, IL: Human Kinetics, 2000

Costas, Bob. *Fair Ball: A Fans Case for Baseball*. New York: Broadway Books, 2000

Dorfman, H.A. *The Mental Keys to Hitting*. Lanham, MD: Diamond Communications, 2001

Kim, Sang H. *Ultimate Flexibility*. Wethersfield, CT: Turtle Press, 2004

Kindall, Jerry and John Winkin. *The Baseball Coaching Bible.* Champaign, IL: Human Kinetics, 2000

Lau Jr., Charley and Jeffrey Flanagan. *Lau's Laws on Hitting.* Lanham, MD: Taylor Trade Publishing, 2003

Lau, Charlie, and Alfred Glossbrenner. *The Art of Hitting .300.* New York: Penguin Books, 1991

Oh, Sadaharu, and David Falkner. *A Zen Way of Baseball.* New York: Times Books, 1984

Winfield, Dave and Eric Swenson. *The Complete Baseball Player.* New York: Avon Books, 1990

Wolff, Rick. *Playing Better Baseball.* Champaign, IL: Human Kinetics, 1997

Dorfman, H.A. and Karl Kuehl. *The Mental Game of Baseball.* Lanham, MD: Diamond Communications, 1989

Rouzier, M.D., Pierre. *The Sports Medicine Patient Advisor.* Amherst, MA: SportsMed Press, 2010

Hyman, Mark. *Until it Hurts.* Boston, MA: Beacon Press, 2009

Dorfman, H.A. *The Mental ABC's of Pitching.* Lanham, MD: Diamond Communications, 2000

Turbow, Jason and Michael Duca. *The Baseball Codes.* New York: Random House, Inc., 2010

Andrews, Dr., James and Don Yaeger. *Any Given Monday.* New York: Scribner, 2013

Acknowledgements

While paddling the peaceful waters of the *Boundary Waters Canoe Area Wilderness* near Ely, Minnesota, good friends Jim Huot-Vickery and Ken MacDonald encouraged me to write about what I had learned on my long journey through youth sports. They have been with me every step of the way—reading chapters, correcting mistakes, imparting wisdom and knowledge, providing clarity, and sharing truths about life's journey. My gratitude for their caring effort is undying.

My wife, Lynn, my daughter, Shelley, and my son, Phillip, have each inspired me in their own special way as I have taken this journey through the world of youth sports, my life, and the writing of this book. Their love and support has sustained this dreamer through the many long hours, months, and years it took to bring this project to fruition.

Garry Shandling—who through a disciplined approach to his own career—taught me what it means to be consistent in order to achieve success, and to follow your honest path.

To my many karate and baseball students and all the kids I have been privileged to have coached, you have been the inspiration for this book.

Brian Schumacher, by sharing his own experience in youth sports, has been a resource for me from day one.

Early on in my coaching career, Greg Gunnells provided much needed instruction and truth about the game of baseball and motivated me to learn more.

Jack Hand of Mid-State Amateur Baseball Association, who through his wisdom and commitment to youth baseball, inspired me to be the best coach I could be. George Grant provided much needed guidance along the way as I wrote the chapters and contemplated how to get them in print.

John Reitmeier has been supporting me with technical advice and friendship as long as I can remember. It has served me well on this project and other areas of my life. I am also very appreciative to Jonathan Motley for legal and business advice.

Thom Barry, Alan Nierob, Julie Nathanson, and Mark Volman generously shared their wisdom, friendship and wit as I made my way through unknown territory in the writing and publishing of this book.

Gratitude and respect to my Sensei, Bob Ozman (1936-2012), whose excellent instruction in Isshinryu karate started me down a path of fitness, enlightenment, and self-discipline that would lead to the youth baseball fields of Middle Tennessee. Our many long conversations have lent perspective when most needed.

Others who deserve thanks include Peter Berg, Jim Rantz, Donavan Haugstad, Mark Warren, Matt Anderson, Gary Gilbert, Marshall Pearson, Mike Ladd, David Kmita, Adam Moore, Pastor Chuck Westra, Charles Pareigis, Donny Nowell, Todd Hyatt, Trevor Scott, and Jordan Dobberstein—all who read several of the chapters and provided helpful comments.

And finally, a special thank you to David Dunham, Joel Dunham, and Crystal Flores of Dunham Books for their professional expertise in taking this project from manuscript to finished book form.

About the Author

Chuck Schumacher is an American karate and baseball instructor born in 1953. He has traveled many paths in his life: professional musician, woodworker, baseball coach, martial artist and baseball instructor. He and Lynn, his wife of 30 years, have raised two children, Shelley and Phillip. They moved to Franklin, Tennessee in 1990 and have lived there for the past 24 years. Chuck spent 20 of those years as a volunteer coach. He has coached all age groups at the rec level, several competitive travel teams, and also served as a Varsity baseball hitting coach.

Teaching baseball and martial arts at his facility, Chucks Gym, Schumacher has become known for his ability to work with young athletes, motivating them to get the most of their ability while developing character traits that will benefit them later in life.

Chuck Schumacher's longtime training in martial arts has resulted in an expert understanding of the movements of an athlete's body. He has been applying this knowledge of movement while teaching the discipline of the mind not only in martial arts, but baseball. The main focus of his teaching and athletic training has been that mind, body and technique are "one," meaning that all must be present and fine-tuned to develop ones full potential.

Coach Chucks way of teaching young athletes to achieve their full potential has been influential for parents as well as youth coaches. The mainstay of his teaching and writing has been to educate parents and coaches of young athletes as to how they can best play their role so kids can enjoy the process of skill development while learning life lessons along the way. The role of the parent in their child's journey through sports, Chuck believes, is crucial to their healthy development as a player and as a person.